MEDIEVAL WEYMOUTH

GROWTH AND DECLINE

MEDIEVAL WEYMOUTH
GROWTH AND DECLINE

JAMES CRUMP

YOUCAXTON PUBLICATIONS

OXFORD & SHREWSBURY

ISBN 978-190964-47-17
Printed and bound in Great Britain.
Published by James Crump 2015

Cover Illustration: *Battle of Sluys* from Jean de Wavrin's Chronicles
of England, Bruges, c. 1461-83, courtesy of the British Library

Acknowledgements

I am indebted to the Dorset History Centre for permission to use the images of the 1318 and 1571 charters and the seal of 1318; also to Weymouth Library for those of the charter of 1252, the letters patent of 1616 and the seals of 1285 and 1592. In addition I would like to thank the staffs of the Dorset History Centre, Weymouth Library, Weymouth Museum and the British Library for their assistance over a long period of time. Last but not least I am grateful to my wife Pauline for casting a critical eye over the text at every stage of its writing and for her computer skills without which I would have been lost.

Contents

Acknowledgements   v

Introduction   1

Origins   3

The Charters   9

Weymouth and Melcombe. Planned Medieval Towns   21

The Growth of the Towns in the
    Thirteenth and Fourteenth Centuries   31

War, disease and decline   38

Religion   54

Town life in the fourteenth century   63

The End of the Middle Ages   73

Endnotes   85

Abbreviations   92

Bibliography   93

Index   99

Introduction

In many respects Weymouth and Melcombe Regis were 'typical' of medieval English towns. They both emerged on the back of the surge of urbanisation that took place from the late thirteenth century onwards and the great medieval trades of wool and wine provided the basis of their economic life. As was the case elsewhere, their feudal lords were the decisive agents in their foundation – both were 'planted' towns – and their charters, granted by their lords, were the instruments of their early development. Melcombe was somewhat unusual in that it was also deliberately planned with a more sophisticated grid layout and analysis of its town plan provides some of the most striking evidence of its medieval past.

Even at the height of their medieval prosperity both were small (as were most medieval towns). They were also lacking in some aspects that might be seen to be characteristics of towns at this time. Melcombe, for example, had no religious provision for many years. From the late fourteenth century they became smaller still and remained so well into the sixteenth century. The reasons for this decline are complex. Contemporaries attached most importance to the effects – economic, financial and physical – of the prolonged conflict with France known as the 'Hundred Years War'. Others, perhaps influenced by Melcombe's notoriety as the 'original' port of entry of the Black Death, have drawn attention to that plague and subsequent epidemics. Most probably, as will be explained later, it was the coincidence of both that proved devastating.

Both towns, but Weymouth particularly, retained what might be thought of as 'medieval' attributes until almost the end of the sixteenth century, especially in their governance. This was primarily the result of their historic rivalry during the preceding centuries which delayed their achieving what by then was coming to be seen as a desirable and inevitable accommodation.

Chapter 1
Origins

The modern town of Weymouth is less than five hundred years old. It was brought into being in 1571 when the two much more ancient boroughs of Weymouth and Melcombe Regis, which had been rivals for years, were merged by Act of Parliament into a single corporation. Even then, it took another twenty years before this legal union of the two old towns was made into a physical union by linking them for the first time by a bridge. Until that time, the only direct means of crossing between them had been by a rope ferry. Resistance to the new constitutional arrangements and their consequences still persisted, however, a legacy of centuries of disputes about rights over the harbour which lay between them. The history of Weymouth, then, before the final quarter of the sixteenth century is the history not of a single town but of two: very different in appearance and jealous of their identities and what they saw to be their rights. However, as will be seen, over the centuries, their stories were essentially similar.

The foundations of Weymouth and Melcombe as towns, or as places which had the potential to become towns, are for the most part to be found in the thirteenth century. This was a time when many towns were being deliberately created in Britain and elsewhere in western Europe. It was a period when general phenomena such as population growth, the development of trade and economic activity, the increasing commercialization of society, the spreading use of money in everyday life and so on were all favouring town growth and creating a climate in which towns could more readily spring up[1]. But this did not happen spontaneously. It was often attempts by institutions and individuals to exploit and profit from that climate which were crucial to the emergence of many particular medieval towns. Usually this key role was played by manorial lords who were seeking to maximize financial returns from their estates and this was the case in both Weymouth and Melcombe. In Weymouth the decisive agents were firstly St. Swithun's Priory, a monastery attached to Winchester Cathedral, and later on the powerful Clare family who were Earls of Gloucester. In Melcombe it was the Crown, initially in the persons of Edward I and his Queen, Eleanor of Castile. Firstly, these town promoters and developers, because that is what they were, would secure market rights and other fiscal and commercial privileges by obtaining (or in the case of the monarchy simply granting) charters to facilitate their projects. Then they set about town development and building activities.

Before the thirteenth century very little is known about the general history of the Weymouth area and what evidence exists has nothing to say directly about the towns themselves. There has been a good deal of speculation about the existence of a Roman harbour and its possible location. It has been variously placed either at the head of Radipole Lake from where it was linked by road to the Roman town of Durnovaria (Dorchester), or at some other spot in the Wey estuary known as the Backwater. There is certainly evidence of Roman occupation around Weymouth with possible villa sites a temple site and cemeteries, and numerous artefacts including a substantial coin hoard have been found. But this has little bearing on the location and development of the two later towns. Similarly, evidence for what might be termed the 'Anglo-Saxon' history of Weymouth - principally charters dating from the tenth and eleventh centuries - reveals little more than the probable existence of a settlement with that name and some hints about activities that may have been carried on there.

The earliest of these charters is one of 934 in which King Athelstan, who was a generous benefactor of monasteries, granted substantial lands in Dorset to Milton Abbey along with river rights at Weymouth[2]. The terms of this grant are said to refer to 'all the water within the shore of Waimouth and half the stream of Waimouth out at sea', although it should be noted that A.D. Mills translates the wording of the charter as 'all the water within the shore (i.e. inshore) from the mouth of the Wey and half the river in the Wey estuary out at sea' and does not specifically mention the town itself[3]. A reference in this grant to victuals ('ad victum') has been taken to mean that a settlement there was supplying the monastery with fish. This may have been an arrangement similar to the one known to have existed more than a century later along the coast where, according to the Domesday Book, a handful of men at Lyme Regis held fishing rights from Sherborne Abbey.

In another charter dated about 988 Aethelred II ('the Redeless', i.e the 'badly-advised') granted to a certain Atsere 'his faithful minister' lands at Uuike (Wyke) near to the island of Portland[4]. The extent of the grant was described in terms of landmarks which are no longer determinable, although 'Lotomor' (Lodmoor) is mentioned. The grant is usually taken to include Weymouth and Melcombe[5]. Indeed, John Hutchins in his history of Dorset claimed that the charter referred to 'that place called by its inhabitants Weymouth or Wick' but neither is mentioned by name and so this charter also cannot be said to provide definitive evidence of settlement there[6]. The document itself is not original but a copy in the Winchester Old Minster archive dating from later than 1250 and some aspects of its authenticity have also been questioned[7].

The third document is a writ of King Edward the Confessor declaring that he has bequeathed Portland and everything belonging thereto to the Old Minster at Winchester. Unfortunately (or fortunately if one likes tall stories) this has become linked to the lurid legend of the ordeal of Queen Emma, Edward's mother[8]. She was the widow of both King Aethelred II and King Cnut, extremely rich and powerful, deeply involved in the dynastic politics of the time and possibly a supporter of the claim of Magnus of Norway to the English throne in preference to her son. In about 1042 her lands and wealth were seized by King Edward who was said to have become 'exasperated' with her politicking. According to the legend much darker reasons were involved. Emma was accused of being implicated in the death of another son, Alfred, of trying to poison yet another, and of 'criminal familiarity' with Alwyn, bishop of Winchester. To vindicate herself Emma agreed to submit to trial by ordeal of fire. In Winchester cathedral, before a large assembly, she walked barefoot and blindfolded over nine red hot ploughshares and emerged unharmed and therefore innocent. In gratitude for this spectacular outcome, the legend says, Emma and Alwyn each gave nine manors (symbolizing the nine ploughshares) to the Winchester church. The King also gave nine manors to the church as a penance. The relevance of all this to Weymouth's history is that four of the manors which appear in a number of tellings and retellings of the legend by chroniclers as having been given by the King were 'Portelond, Wikes, Helwell and Waimuth'. However, none of these manors were recorded as belonging to the Winchester Minster in the Domesday Survey of 1086 and in spite of its appearance in many chronicles there is no reliable contemporary source for the events of the legend. The writ itself simply declares that the King had bequeathed Portland and everything belonging thereto to the Minster. The other three manors were later frequently linked with Portland and this is probably how they came to be involved in accounts of the legend. This is borne out by a charter of Henry I of around 1106 which declared that the monks of St. Swithun hold the manor of Portland, which King Edward had given to them together with Wike and the ports of Waimuth and Melecumbe with all their appurtenances and rights of wreck and all their liberties and free customs by sea and land. Interestingly, it concludes by saying that these liberties were granted 'just as they had ever had the benefit of them'[9]. This suggests that the association had already been made.

The Angevin Empire
Map of the French lands of the English crown in the reign of
Henry II, 1154-1189

Neither town appears in the Domesday Survey. Although there are several references to Dorset manors whose names contain the element Wai(a), none can be definitely associated with Weymouth itself. Melcombe is not mentioned, although the manor of Radipole which contained it is listed as belonging to Cerne Abbey. The only other local Domesday reference is to Brige(a) which appears to have been a small fishing settlement in the neighbourhood of Wyke Regis. The probability is that by the end of the tenth century Weymouth at least existed as a small fishing settlement with monastic connections. Perhaps something similar was taking place at Melcombe, but there is no record of it. All that can be said of the Anglo-Saxon history of Weymouth, therefore, is that it is speculative and the evidence for it circumstantial.

It was events in the eleventh century which made the difference. Undoubtedly the most important influence on the early growth of the two ports was the development of links with France after the Norman Conquest of 1066 and especially those with south central and south western France after the bringing together of the lands of Normandy and of the Counts of Anjou by Henry II and then his marriage to Eleanor of Aquitaine in 1152. Clearly both towns were operating as ports by the beginning of the twelfth century when they were described as such in the charter of Henry I already mentioned. Later, during the reign of Henry II this grant was reconfirmed, although in this case Melcombe was not referred to as a port.

However, by 1224 almost all the lands of the so-called Angevin Empire had been lost to the French kings, Only Aquitaine with Bordeaux and Bayonne and their hinterland of Gascony still belonged to the English crown. But it was trade with these areas which had given Weymouth and Melcombe their start and it was to remain of lasting importance to them. Gascon wine was England's most significant import at this time and the return trade of wool, cloth and grain were all commodities which were vital to the two towns throughout the middle ages. As yet, however, even by medieval standards the towns were still small and insignificant as ports and they remained so until the second half of the thirteenth century.

Chapter 2.
The Charters

In medieval documents places are sometimes referred to by the term 'vill' signifying a township, sometimes by 'burgus' meaning borough. Both have been used at different times during the middle ages to describe Weymouth and Melcombe; but neither gives any precise idea of the size or status or character of the towns. In fact, during the medieval past there were places which were referred to as boroughs which never developed into proper towns and, conversely, there were places which were clearly functioning as towns long before they became formal boroughs[10]. This was the case with both Weymouth and Melcombe which are known to have been represented as 'burgi' (boroughs) at Courts of Assize - in 1244 and 1268 respectively - before they gained formal borough status[11]. However, the granting of that status and the institutions and privileges that accompanied it was a decisive change. Weymouth was given it by monastic charter in 1252 and Melcombe by royal charter in 1280 and from these two dates their histories as towns can be said to have properly begun.

In the middle ages there were different kinds of town charters. They could be granted by the crown or by magnates, both lay and ecclesiastical, the main differences between the two types being that royal charters could grant a wider range of privileges and lords usually tried to preserve more powers for themselves. They could be used by manorial lords simply to obtain rights for places on their estates to hold markets or fairs and there are early examples of this type in the history of Weymouth. For instance, in 1248 John de Cauz, Prior of St. Swithun's Winchester which held the lordship of the manor of Wyke, obtained a charter granting the right to hold a weekly market and a yearly fair in Weymouth[12]. This was regranted in 1251, possibly with additional privileges[13]. More far-reachingly, charters could be used to create boroughs and endow them with valuable rights: notably allowing the burgesses freedom of tenure, a court separate from the manorial court and freedom from tolls. Weymouth's next charter in 1252 was such a one[14].

The Weymouth Charter of 1252
The remains of the charter granted to Weymouth
by William of Taunton.

On July 17, 1252, the recently-installed Prior of St. Swithun's, William of Taunton, granted Weymouth a new charter. Its terms make it clear that the Prior was indeed trying to promote Weymouth in the interests of his own convent. Exactly what kind of future

William had in mind is not spelled out, but it was obviously intended to be more than that of a small market town serving the local population south of the Ridgeway. His hope certainly was that it would grow in size and expand its maritime trade and this can be seen from the terms of the charter. Exactly what the area was to which it applied, and therefore what was considered at the time to be the extent of the town of Weymouth, cannot be determined because the boundaries of the town were described by reference to landmarks which cannot now be recognized: some were the properties of named individuals such as 'the house of Thomas Engelram', 'the land of William of Bromdon', or 'the hedge of Gilbert of Wycumb'; while others such as 'la Hopehus' (the house at the Ope - the present Hope Square) are recognizable but give only a general idea.

The charter began by declaring that 'our port of Waymue' shall be free for ever and open for anyone to trade there, subject to paying to the Priory the usual customs due. The town was to be a 'free borough' ('liber burgus') in which the burgesses held their properties by 'burgage tenure'; that is they had the right freely to sell, exchange, bequeath or devise their burgage plots and other tenements. The burgesses were also freed from all import duties and were to have all the privileges of the towns of Portsmouth and Southampton. The inhabitants of Weymouth and their families were set free from servile status and allowed to move and trade freely. No tallages or aids (types of taxation) were to be levied on the borough (even by the king) unless they were urgently needed by the church at Winchester, or by the crown by common consent of the whole kingdom.

What is clear from these terms is that the Priory was seeking to make the town grow and to attract inhabitants by offering them security of tenure, free status and the chance of prospering by reducing the burdens placed upon them. At the same time it was trying to enlarge the port's trade by encouraging all comers, whilst giving its own merchants privileges and making sure they were not disadvantaged in relation to bigger ports such as Southampton and Portsmouth. The town's inhabitants were also given additional 'sweeteners'. For example, the 'amercement' (fine) for breaches of the assize of ale (a common offence) was to be limited to fourpence payable to the Priory; and if the Priory decided to 'seize' any goods for itself, then the price it would pay would be 'better by one penny in twelve pennyworths' than it could be sold for elsewhere', the specific example of goods given is naturally fish.

The benefits to the Priory of these arrangements would come in the form of the rents at which the burgages had been valued, together with customs payments and fines from the borough court; all of which were to be paid to the town's bailiffs twice yearly. The bailiffs themselves were to be chosen by the burgesses, but they were required to do fealty to the Prior and Convent, and they were accountable to the latter for all pleas, quarrels, wrecks, advantages and profits which accrued from the town to the Priory. Courts were to be held in the town, presided over by the Priory's seneschal or other bailiff, with the amount of amercements being decided by four of the burgesses of the town according to the seriousness of the offence. The court would 'do justice to all', but also guard the Priory's interests. Weymouth burgesses could not be made to plead in other courts about Weymouth matters, except for pleas relating to the crown, or where the borough court could be shown to have failed to do justice. This protected the burgesses from interference in town affairs from other courts. These provisions give a good impression of what the business life of the town would have been like in the second half of the thirteenth century, although large allowances need to be made for the corruption, manipulation of the court by influential burgesses and general malfeasance endemic at the time.

Melcombe's original charter was more impressive and was granted by King Edward I in 1280. The original has been lost and its terms are only known because they were recited in a later 'charter of inspeximus' (inspection) of King Edward II in 1318[15].

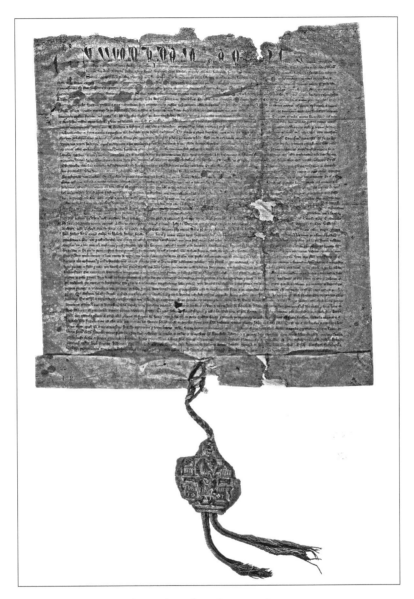

The Melcombe Charter of 1318
This is a charter of 'inspeximus' (inspection) and confirmation of
the lost charter of Edward I of 1280 which it repeats 'in hec verba'
(in these words). It was granted by Edward II in 1318 and goes on
to make additional provisions of its own.
(DHC DWM CH1 2)

Unlike the Weymouth charter it does not declare that Melcombe is a 'free borough' but instead assumes it. It is addressed to 'our burgesses of Melcombe' and contains explicit references to the 'burgus' and the 'portsoke' (the areas outside the boundaries of the borough where the inhabitants were subject to the jurisdiction of its court). This chimes with other evidence which, as has been shown, suggests that 'borough-like' activity had been going on in Melcombe for some time which was now taken a stage further and formalized.

What was new and most significant in this charter was that the Melcombe burgesses were granted all the liberties which had been granted by the crown to the city of London. Most crucially Melcombe was to have its own court (like London a 'hustings court' meeting weekly, unlike the local hundred court which met monthly) where all matters affecting the property and business of the burgesses would be settled. The burgesses could not be called before other courts in such matters. Also, to assist the court by reducing formalities and making allowance for inexperience, the charter provided that no-one should be penalized for what was known as 'miskenning' -i.e. getting procedures wrong in making a plea or stating the facts of a case, which otherwise might have resulted in a fine or forfeiture of the case by the pleader. Provisions like this were designed to make business easier and faster and freer from outside interference. Next, the legal rights of the burgesses to their lands, tenures sureties and debts were confirmed according to the custom of London. They were even allowed to enrol their debts in the royal exchequer on payment of one penny in the pound, giving them extra security. The jurisdiction of the borough court did not extend, however, to 'pleas belonging to the crown' such as offences against the peace which were subject to common law, nor could the court try the king's moneyers or officers.

The charter went on to give the Melcombe burgesses freedom from all toll and lastage (levies on merchandise, lastage being on ships' cargoes) and all customs at all ports throughout the king's dominions. An exception to this wide-ranging privilege was the ancient royal right to 'wine prise' by which the crown was entitled to two tuns of wine from every cargo (or an equivalent twenty shillings per tun after this was commuted to a money tax).

While Melcombe men were thus given advantages which applied throughout the king's lands, 'foreigners' (i.e. people from outside the borough) who came to trade were subjected to restrictions there. Anyone trying to do business outside the borough and thus avoiding its tolls was liable to imprisonment or forfeiture of goods and any traders who owed customs were not allowed to display their wares. Merchant strangers and 'our Jews', the charter said, were specifically excluded from its provisions and would be dealt with as seemed expedient to the crown. ('Our Jews', who had for many years financed royal projects and been virtually bankrupted in the process, thus becoming useless, were expelled from England in 1290).

The charter then relieved the inhabitants of Melcombe from a whole collection of feudal obligations and aspects of manorial control. Similar provisions appear in a number of other charters and so were not special or specific to Melcombe and some of the burdens were declining in importance. Nevertheless others were onerous and resented. And so the inhabitants of Melcombe were released from 'murdrum', a fine imposed on the whole community when a murderer could not be captured; they were no longer to be liable to 'duellum', which was trial by combat, and the king's marshals could not forcibly billet royal officers or servants on them. They could no longer be fined by a lord for the offence of 'childewite', by fathering a child on one of his bondwomen; they were freed from 'yeresgive', the obligation under certain circumstances to make gifts to a lord, and the Melcombe bailiffs (or anyone else) were forbidden to make a 'scotale', which was a tax on ale, which might also have involved compelling people to buy the lord's ale at an inflated price. This was greatly resented and seems to have led to popular protests in some places. Today these details of the charter seem archaic and remote. But to the people of the time they meant a great deal. In their eyes, going to live in the town meant freedom from manorial control and opportunities at least to better themselves and prosper. Creating this impression was part of the purpose of all these clauses, which was to attract people into the town.

After reciting and confirming the terms of 1280 the remainder of Edward II's 1318 charter was entirely specific to Melcombe and

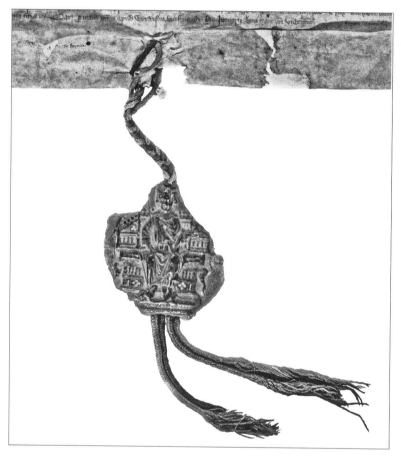

The seal of the Melcombe Charter of 1318
(DHC DWM CH1 2)

contained a number of interesting and important details, both about the operation of the medieval borough and the physical shape of the town itself. Firstly, it stated that the borough was held by 'fee farm'. This was a fixed amount which the burgesses would pay into the Exchequer in return for their holdings and for the privilege of collecting the revenues of both the borough and the port and retaining them. In the terminology of the age, the burgesses had made a 'fine' with the king i.e. an agreement to pay a lump sum of eight marks per year, which was, the charter said, an increase of two marks on 'what they used to pay', the value of the mark being thirteen shillings and fourpence. In return for this increase in the fee farm the King granted the burgesses seven pieces of empty land on which they might build, or let or sell. Two were on St. Edmund Street, three on Bakerestrete, one on St. Thomas Street and one between St. Thomas Street and St. Mary Street.. The empty land granted amounted to seventy one square perches, equivalent to approximately two thousand one hundred and forty eight square yards (less than half an acre) and had an annual value in 1318 of one shilling and one penny.

These grants of land are informative in a number of ways. They provide the first documentary reference to these street names. Bakerestrete is a name which has been lost but which most probably followed a street line which has had a number of name changes and is now known as St. Alban's Street, since one at least of these parcels of land is described as being on the northern side of Bakerestrete, implying that the street ran east to west. The medieval street plan shows no other possiblity between St. Edmund Street and the town ditch , since Bakerestrete was obviously part of the original grid of streets in 1318 and not an extension of it. These grants of empty land also show that the grid had not yet filled up with holdings. Finally, this charter provided that there should be a weekly market on Monday (instead of Tuesday as previously) and a fair lasting eight days around St. Botolph's day (17 June).

These charters were confirmed again by King Edward III at the beginning of his reign in 1328. Towns often thought it wise to obtain (and pay for) a renewal of their rights on the accession of a new sovereign and this happened a number of times in the case of Melcombe.

The benefits to the budding towns of charters like this are obvious. They were given rights and privileges which were valuable and crucial to their development. What is perhaps less obvious is that similar advantages also accrued to the crown and manorial lords as a result of granting such charters. A market or a town was seen by them as a means of converting various rights and dues invested in manorial lordship into the monetary values of rents, taxes and fines; or as places where they could secure through tolls a share in the profits of increasing trade. All this can be clearly seen in these early charters of Weymouth and Melcombe.

The nature of these charters and the evidence of subsequent documents make it clear that from the outset there were distinct differences in status between the boroughs of Weymouth and Melcombe. These would lead to a succession of problems and disputes between the two towns which lasted for centuries. Weymouth originated as a seigneurial borough (i.e. created by a manorial lord) and retained a structure of manorial courts presided over by stewards and bailiffs (but with major concessions in terms of the liberties and rights of tenants intended to favour their trading activities) until the union of the boroughs in 1571. Weymouth's first incorporation was in 1571; this was confirmed in 1598 and then it was reincorporated in 1616. On the other hand, Melcombe was first incorporated in the lost charter of 1280 which was confirmed in 1318, 1328 and 1461. Incorporation was essentially a royal grant. As has been shown, there was only a handful of seigneurial incorporations[16].

The implications of this were spelled out as early as 1333 in an Inquisition of the reign of Edward III. This stated that half the port belonged to each respective town with petty customs from ships,

Melcombe Borough Seal, 1285
This is the earliest surviving seal of the borough of Melcombe,
dating from about 1285. The inscription reads 'sigillum comunie
de Melcoma' (the common seal of Melcombe). The shields show
the arms of the Kingdom of Leon quartered with those of Castile,
a reference to Edward I's wife, Eleanor of Castile, who was the
daughter of Ferdinand III of Castile. At either end of the ship is a
sprig of broom, or planta genista,
a reference to the motif of the Plantagenets.

barks and vessels arriving and unloading on either side together
with divers other rents, profits and commodities, for mills, cartage
and other things *'by charter and grant in fee farm held to the town
of Melcombe and without charter and grant in fee farm, but at the
King's pleasure, at an annual rent or farm of 40s. to that of Weymouth'.*

Elizabethan documents also habitually refer to the burgesses and inhabitants of Weymouth as tenants and, as in the inquisition of 1333, insist that their entitlement to petty customs and harbour dues on their side is 'without charter or grant in fee farm and but at her Majesty's will and pleasure' and that the 'burgesses and tenants of Weymouth have held the same at the will of her Majesty and her noble progenitors paying only a rent or farm of 40s. for the same, by the year, time out of mind'[17].

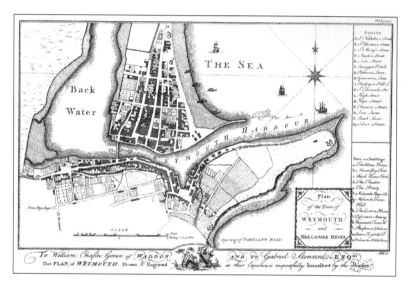

Map of Weymouth and Melcombe Regis
From J. Hutchins, 'The History and Antiquities of
the County of Dorset', 1ˢᵗ. edition, 1774

Chapter 3
Weymouth and Melcombe.
Planned Medieval Towns

Often the granting of a charter to a town was simply the first part of a three-stage process which was quickly followed by the laying out of streets and building plots and then by attempts to attract immigrants - merchants, traders and craftsmen - to take them up. This certainly happened in Melcombe in the 1280's and most probably some time earlier in Weymouth also. The second stage can be seen from an analysis of the plans of both towns. However, the radically different physical features of the sites on either side of the harbour made those plans look very different.

Weymouth (more accurately, of course, Weymouth and Melcombe Regis) is fortunate in having three good contemporary descriptions, dating from each of the sixteenth, seventeenth and eighteenth centuries. These show what the town was like before it turned itself away from its ancient focus on the harbour and towards a more expansive future oriented towards the Esplanade and the beach. They give a picture of the town which had changed little since the middle ages..

The latest of the three accounts was that of John Hutchins whose history of Dorset, written in the 1770's, noted that, in the case of Weymouth, in his day the narrowness of the ground between the harbour and a steep hill rising on the south meant that the town *'contains but one narrow and irregular street, near a mile in length, which runs east and west and another that runs north to south to the Look Out. The houses are of stone and tiled; but generally low and indifferent'*. This rather cursory description is somewhat contradicted, however, by the map he commissioned for his book which shows a slightly more developed street system. In contrast, he thought that Melcombe on the other side of the harbour, *'much surpasses Weymouth for the convenience and pleasantness of its situation'*; and although, he continued, it stands on a peninsula and can only be entered through a narrow isthmus, it has a more extensive and flat site. *'It has two streets, broad and well paved, which terminate in a spacious market place. Many of the houses are large and high, though in general low, as are most of the buildings in this county near the sea and are of stone and tiled. Here are also many houses and yards for wares[18].'*

Hutchins' remarks follow closely those of Thomas Gerard writing almost a century and a half earlier (in a work generally known as Coker's 'Survey of Dorsetshire') who drew attention to the same features. *'Weymouth as nowe it is, is but little, consisting chiefelie of one streete, which for a good space lyeth open to the Sea, and on the back of it riseth an hill of such steepnesse that they are forced to climbe up to their chappell by sixty steppes of stone'.* Whereas *'Melcombe on the other side...much surpasseth the other for conveniencie of scite, for this standing on a Flatte affordeth room for Buildings with a Market Place, and convenient Streetes, and also Yardes for their wares by meanes whereof the Marchants have chosen this for their habitation, which of late Yeares is fairelie newe built[19].'*

About a hundred years earlier still John Leland in his 'Itinerary' had also noted the site features of what he called the *'tounlets'*. In Weymouth he draws attention to *'a key and a warf for shippes'* and notes the proximity of this to *'the haven mouth almost at hand'*. He comments on the quality of houses in Melcombe, which *'be welle and stronglie bilded of stone'*. Leland considered that Weymouth was the larger town, although Melcombe *'as yt ys evidently seene, hath beene far bigger than yt is now[20]*.

The earliest towns were even smaller than Leland's 'tounlets' In Melcombe the original nucleus of the town was probably in the south western corner of the present town site at the end of St. Nicholas Street. The southern end of this street and Lower St. Edmund Street, which follows a line markedly different from the present-day course of St. Edmund Street suggests a simple configuration of the town, located on the early quayside here. The ferry or *'trajectus...by a bote and rope, bent over the haven, so that yn the ferry bote they use no ores'* described by Leland also linked Weymouth with Melcombe at the end of St. Nicholas Street[21].

It is difficult to locate the original nucleus of Weymouth with any precision. The vagueness of the earliest description of the early town's boundaries contained in the charter of 1252 has already been mentioned. The only reference it contains which is of any value in this respect is to 'la hopehus' (usually rendered as 'the house on the inlet or cove')[22]. This is often taken to indicate that early settlement developed around Hope Cove[23] and there was clearly activity there be the end of the sixteenth century. Equally vague is a map of the Dorset coast of 1539[24] which shows no houses around the cove; but what it does show is a group of buildings by the ferry, which accords with Leland's description c.1538 in which Weymouth is said to lie 'strait agayn Milton [Melcombe]... and at this place [is] the trajectus'. The 1539 map also shows another group of houses further west of this.

Both Weymouth and Melcombe have been described as 'planned' medieval 'new towns' which were 'planted' at some stage during the thirteenth century[25]. Clearly, the process of 'plantation' did not begin with empty sites but was a development grafted onto the already existing, albeit small, beginnings which have just been described. How such a plantation came about can best be explained by using the case of Melcombe which at the time was held up as an example in the instructions given by the King to be used for the creation of a new port at Newton in Studland in 1286. At Newton the individuals who were actually to carry out the project are known. King Edward I, who was then at Exeter, appointed Sir Richard de

Bosco, the Constable of Corfe Castle, and a cleric, Walter de Marisco, to supervise the laying out of a new town. They were told that it should have sufficient streets and lanes, building plots for merchants and others and sites for a market, a church and a harbour. Eventually, like Melcombe, it was also to have a royal charter with similar terms. In the end, nothing came of this plan. New town proposals could fail as well as succeed[26].

What happened in Melcombe was very different. In 1280, the Abbot of Cerne, lord of the manor of Radipole, had asserted a claim to hold a market and fair in Melcombe, which was part of that manor, by virtue of a charter of King Henry III. According to Hutchins 'not long after, that convent parted with it to the crown and it became part of the dowry of Elianor [sic], Queen of King Edward I on whose account great privileges were granted to it[27].' This was obviously so because immediately after the Abbot's grant Melcombe was given its charter and the King and his wife, Eleanor of Castile, both of whom were experienced town promoters in Gascony and Wales as well as England, set in train its growth.

The best evidence for what happened next is to be found in the present street system of the town which dates from this time and suggests a quite sophisticated approach to its planning. One of the most striking and unusual things about the medieval plan of Melcombe is that it has two parallel principal streets, St. Thomas Street and St. Mary Street. This layout has obviously to do with the town's peninsular site which the medieval planners were trying to make the most of. This simple alignment facilitated rapidity of surveying and layout. But, most importantly, ,it gave easy, direct access from the landward entrances to the town (whatever arrangements existed for crossing the town ditch, which was the northern boundary) to the quay and market place. The two main streets were crossed at right angles by two others, St. Edmund Street and another (probably Bakerestrete as has been suggested earlier) to form the orthogonal grid which can still be seen today.

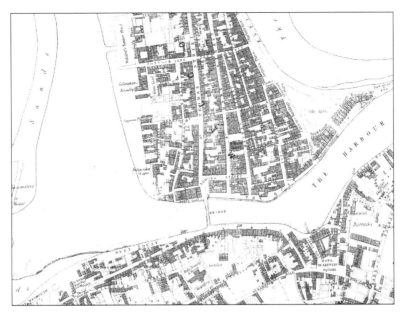

*Map of Melcombe and Weymouth
(Reproduced from the 1859 Ordnance Survey)*

At the southern end lay the 'spacious market place' described by Hutchins and Gerard several centuries later. This fronted present-day St. Edmund Street and probably involved the removal of an earlier street closer to the quayside ending in present -day Lower St. Edmund Street, showing also how this later replanning of the town in 1280 cut across the earlier configuration.

Medieval Melcombe was thus divided into rectangular blocks. This is still apparent in modern street maps, early town guides and even more so in large scale nineteenth century ordnance survey maps and the town plan in Hutchins. In turn, these blocks had been laid out into parcels of land known as 'burgage plots' - i.e. the separate properties which would be owned by the burgesses who took them up. Characteristically, these plots were rectangular and much longer than they were wide and were set at right angles to the streets to maximise the available, valuable street frontage. In the thirteenth century, as now, the principal tenement building, whatever it was, would have been placed at the street end of the plot, perhaps with its gable facing the street and behind there would have been a substantial yard or 'backsides' containing domestic buildings or workshops or gardens. Once established this distinctive pattern of property boundaries has proved to be extremely enduring. In Melcombe the traces of these plots can be seen most clearly on the 1859 O.S. map and even more distinctively on a map based on a survey of holdings made in 1617 and reconstructed from town rentals, leases and later cadastral maps[28]. These show the rectangular plots running east to west between St. Thomas Street and St. Nicholas Street and rather more compact ones between St. Mary Street and Maiden Street (which were probably laid out later than the end of the thirteenth century). Those in the most important central block between St. Thomas Street and St. Mary Street are divided down a rough centre line to give the greatest usage from the frontages of these two principal streets. Plots on St. Edmund Street can be seen to run north to south for the same reason and probably originally fronted onto the market place and quayside.

The work of laying out the town was carried out by surveyors sometimes known as 'locatores'[29] and traces of their work can still be found. It is clear that they used the standard medieval perch of 16ft. 6ins. as their unit of measurement. This can be seen from the documents. The empty plot sizes mentioned in the 1318 charter are all described in terms of this unit. The two plots mentioned in St. Edmund Street and the three mentioned in 'Bakerestrete' were two perches wide and had lengths of two, three, five and ten perches. The one described as being on the west side of St. Thomas Street and that lying between St. Thomas Street and St. Mary Street were each three perches wide and four perches long, (half the width of the central block). It is still possible to find traces of this unit on the ground. Measured along the line of what is now St. Alban's Street the central block of burgage tenements is still

eight perches wide. On the west side of St. Thomas Street south
of St. Alban's Street there are a number of plots which have widths
of one or one and a half perches and even more can be found in
the central section of St. Mary Street on the west side. These have
widths of one or one and a half perches up to three and a half. The
lengths of the plots seem to have been mostly four or five perches,
but they were variable, especially between St. Thomas Street and
St. Nicholas Street and also between St. Mary Street and Maiden
Street, probably responding to topographic features.

St. Nicholas Street may have originated in the early (pre-1280)
town as the road from the north across the 'Narrows' to the original
quayside. The name is first recorded in the catalogue of Ancient
Deeds[30] in 1371 and the neighbourhood, the 'Vico Sancti Nicolai'
in 1373, which suggests that it was later developed northwards
from the old quay site as far as the town ditch (present day Bond
Street) where it ends abruptly, the ancient road presumably having
been blocked at the end of the thirteenth century. Starting from the
quayside the street bends eastward until it reaches Lower St. Alban
Street (Petticoat Lane on early maps) and tenements between it and
St. Thomas Street appear to accommodate to this line, indicating
the earlier presence of the road. From there it follows a straight
course parallel to St. Thomas Street as far as the ditch. The first
mentions of Maiden Street (1379, 1396-8) occur at roughly the
same time and it also ends at the line of the ditch. These two streets
may have developed during the fourteenth century as occupation
lanes giving access to the backs of tenements on the west side and
east side of St. Thomas Street and St. Mary Street respectively.

The entire area of the medieval town south of the town ditch
cannot have consisted of much more than 18 acres, with the
effective original core being about 11 acres. Even then, as is clear
from the 1318 charter, there was empty land in the core. Evidence
from later town leases suggests that the area between St Alban
Street and the town ditch remained largely undeveloped until the

mid-sixteenth century[31]. The main purpose of the town ditch was not defensive, but rather to define the boundary of the privileged urban community which lay beyond it. Once traders crossed it they were subject to the borough's tolls and market regulations and the jurisdiction of its court.

What can be seen, then, from this analysis of the Melcombe town plan is evidence of its systematic development as a new town and it soon became clear that the royal promoters of Melcombe were determined to see their project succeed. Almost from the start the activities of their bailiffs brought them into conflict with the people of Weymouth on the opposite side of the harbour. In 1284 Queen Eleanor brought a suit against one Hugh Cole 'and many more' alleging that since 1282 they had been interfering with the legitimate activities of the Melcombe burgesses as they went about their work of establishing the town, which included the bringing in of stone from Portland 'for making and repairing their buildings'. The Weymouth men were accused of drowning a Melcombe man and of sinking a ship carrying stone[32]. This quarrel was not the first and would certainly not be the last of the disputes between the two towns.

When and how Weymouth began its development as a planned town is not as clear as what happened in Melcombe in the 1280's. It probably started somewhat earlier in the middle of the thirteenth century when it gained its charters. William of Taunton or his agents may have begun the process. But William was expelled from his office of Prior of St. Swithun's in 1255 by Aymer de Valence, bishop of Winchester, and by 1256 William had moved on to become Abbot of Milton. Shortly afterwards c. 1259 the town of Weymouth passed to the powerful Clare family, Earls of Gloucester, by exchange with Winchester[33] and remained in their hands for more than a century. The Clares were inveterate founders and promoters of towns and Weymouth certainly benefited from the connection with them over the long term, so their agents may also have been

Map of Weymouth showing the high street layout and market area.
(Reproduced from the 1864 Ordnance Survey)

involved[34]. Maps and evidence on the ground once again, however, suggest what kind of development it was.

Hutchins' map of 1774, the town plans provided in early nineteenth century guides and the 1859 25-inch ordnance survey map all show the strong and lasting effect of the cliff on the shape of the town plan and demonstrate that Weymouth's earliest form of town plan was the most common one of a single street, running from the quay to the market, place with burgage plots arranged on either side. The 1864 map shows a characteristically triangular market area at the western end of High Street and lying in front of the old town hall where the roads from the villages on the west side of the River Wey - Wyke Regis, Fleet, Chickerell and Radipole - come into the town. This was also a common feature of the so-called 'high street layout' form of town plan. In many medieval towns the buildings and activities associated with a market place are distinctive. Market places were normally where disciplinary functions such as pillories, stocks and frequently prisons were located. If a borough had a town hall it was often to be found here[35]. This was certainly the case in Weymouth. The old Weymouth town hall fronted onto the market place and the lower part of Weymouth town hall was the town prison.[36] This simple plan expanded later when, at the turn of the fourteenth century, Love Lane and Franchise Street made a modest grid with the High Street; but in planning terms, nothing was going on in Weymouth at the end of the thirteenth century comparable either in scale or form to what was happening in Melcombe.

Chapter 4

The Growth of the Towns in the Thirteenth and Fourteenth Centuries

For a new town to grow and succeed it had to attract incomers. Weymouth and Melcombe's charters provided incentives for people from the neighbourhood to move in once the town planners had set out the necessary infrastructure and the building plots where they could settle. In Melcombe, by the beginning of the fourteenth century, this strategy was working and bringing in migrants. This can be seen from the records of the names of the individuals to whom King Edward II committed the administration of Melcombe's fee farm in 1308 and who were therefore already significant burgesses. Of the eight named persons who were made responsible, the names of five indicate where they had come from: Gilbert de Portesham, John de Portland, Robert de Beymistre, Edward de Waye and John de Flete[37]. Somewhat later in 1332 the returns for a tax known as a lay subsidy show that this was continuing with the names of William de Lym and Thomas de Preston occurring on the Melcombe side and in Weymouth John Flete, John Chikerel, Beatrice atte Wolle and Henry atte Wolle[38]. At roughly the same time the accounts of the Earls of Clare show that there were 260 burgage plots in Weymouth in 1329-30, which produced a revenue of £20. 12s. 9d[39].

What activities these people were involved in and what was the exact nature and volume of the trade that was passing through the two ports at this time is difficult to estimate. During the middle ages both participated in the two greatest medieval English trades, the export of wool and the import of wine: Melcombe especially in the export of raw wool and then cloth; Weymouth especially in the import of wine from western France.

It has to be said, however, that at the end of the thirteenth century the scale of their involvement in the wool trade was insignificant. At this time almost all the main wool exporting ports were on the east coast. On the south coast only Southampton was of any consequence, the other southern ports contributing only a minute fraction of the customs revenues for wool[40]. Melcombe's involvement in the trade began to increase during the fourteenth century, however. This came about because of the crown's growing need to increase its revenues. The customs on wool were the most important source of these and this led the crown to direct trade through certain 'staple' towns so that the customs dues could be controlled and collected more effectively. By 1331 Melcombe had become one of these towns and benefited accordingly. There are records of the names of the collectors of customs and in that year Gilbert de Portesham and William de Mareschall fulfilled these roles as well as serving as members of parliament for the borough. From 1336 onwards, however, King Edward III continually increased the duties on exported wool to pay for his wars, with damaging effects on the trade. It appears that, despite this, during the first half of the fourteenth century Melcombe held onto its position and continued to be favoured by the crown. By an Act of Parliament of 1361/2 a staple was ordered to be kept at 'New Melcombe', evidently in addition to the ten English 'home staples' which had been established by the Statute of the Staple of 1354. In 1363, however, only two years after Melcombe was given this status, the Calais staple was established giving dominance in the trade to the London-based Company of the Staple. Some home staples remained, keeping their courts for the recovery of debts and dealing with other pleas as well as continuing to export wool[41]. Melcombe's position was confirmed by yet another Act of Parliament in 1364/5 and so it managed to maintain its involvement in the trade. By this time the export of raw wool was declining because of the onerous burden of duties, but English cloth was beginning to gain an increasing share of European markets and in 1365 Melcombe was additionally a centre for the collection of the customs on cloth. The town was also involved in the trade in grain. Netley Abbey was storing grain in Melcombe at the beginning of the fourteenth century and William Welyfed, 'King's Merchant of Melcombe' was importing grain from Gascony[42]. There are also frequent references in the reign of King Edward III to the export of wheat from Melcombe and to its role as a passage port to France[43].

Customs records show that Weymouth also had some involvement in the wool trade, but more important was its import of Gascon wine. Henry de Thornhull and Arnold Gilliam were collectors of wine duties in Weymouth and Wareham between 1310 and 1313. In this respect, just as the crown favoured Melcombe in the wool trade, so the Clare family promoted the wine trade in Weymouth and appear to have been instrumental in securing for the town its appointment as a staple for French wines. The question of what was the market for Weymouth's wine imports is an interesting one. The trade was risky. Many things could go wrong both with the commodity itself and with its shipment. It was therefore expensive and its consumption restricted to the wealthy. Apart from the Clares themselves, the probability is that there was a significant demand from the large number of monastic houses within easy reach of the port.

Both Weymouth and Melcombe appear at different times in the lists of 'head ports' for customs collection (both wool and wine) between 1275 and 1400 and this is often regarded as a mark of their trading importance[44]. From early in the reign of King Edward I the term 'port' was acquiring an administrative significance denoting a particular coastal town which had customs officials who exercised a supervisory role over a particular stretch of coastline. In 1303, for example, Weymouth seems to have been operating as 'head port' for a stretch which extended as far as Plymouth[45]. Later, in 1320,

Thomas Fardeyn and Henry Lovecok were appointed collectors of the 'customs of wools etc in the vill of Weymouth and all places by the sea coasts unto Plymuth'. The status differences between 'head ports', 'member ports' and 'creeks' was coming to refer to essentially administrative activity and did not necessarily depend on the volume of trade, however.

There must have been a substantial coasting trade in many commodities in both ports[46]. They were the only harbour towns for the long stretch of the Dorset coast of fifty miles or so from Poole to Lyme. Some idea of the hinterland served by the ports at this time can be gained from the findings of an Inquisition into the state of Melcombe in 1408 which reported that the 'dwellers in the counties of Dorset, Somerset and Wiltshire who used to have their victuals and other necessaries in the town' would suffer if the town was not helped to recover from the problems it was having at that time[47].

An impression of the early progress of the towns can be gained from the returns of the lay subsidy tax of 1332. While the returns are of little value for attempting to assess the size of their populations, they give an indication of their wealth and social structure. The table below compares a number of Dorset towns based on average assessments and is particularly revealing[48].

Town	Individuals assessed	Total town assessment	Average assessment
Melcombe	30	£9. 0s. 6d.	6s.
Weymouth	32	£6. 1s. 6d.	3s. 10d.
Lyme Regis	35	£8. 3s. 6d.	4s. 8d.
Bridport	44	£9. 0s. 4d.	4s. 1d.
Shaftesbury	104	£18. 19s. 9d.	3s. 6d.
Dorchester	53	£8. 15s. 11d.	3s. 4d.
Dorset	7621	£771. 1s.11d.	2s..

What the table does not show is that Weymouth, followed by Lyme and then Melcombe, contained the most highly assessed individuals in the county and that Weymouth and Melcombe were dominated by two comparatively very wealthy men. Henry Shoydon paid 40s. in Weymouth, 30s. in Melcombe and also 10s. in Wyke making him the most highly assessed individual in the whole of Dorset. Richard Langynow paid 30s. in Melcombe and 10s. in Weymouth. These two individuals, therefore, paid almost half the total assessment in Weymouth and a third in Melcombe. This puts them on the same level as some of the richest merchants in Southampton[49]. This aspect of the concentration of wealth in the two towns can be pursued further. If one adds to it the total assessments of seven other members of the Langynow family in Melcombe (£2. 4s. 4d.) and that of Cristina Welyfed (30s.) a member of another important mercantile family, these three families paid three quarters of Melcombe's total..The impression that emerges is of two small ports dominated by a very few rich merchants.

So far as the vessels used by these merchants and others operating out of the ports are concerned there is some documentary evidence of their number, size and type. The most reliable indication of the composition of a fleet belonging to either at a particular time is that given in a petition from Melcombe of the first year of the reign of King Henry IV (1399). It relates that 'in King Edward's time' - i.e. the mid-fourteenth century, which was the peak of the town's medieval trading activity - 'there used to be...18 large ships and 6 barges fit for merchandise and there were 40 boats for fishing'[50]. This shows the balance of day-to-day operations.

Some lists exist which name the different types of vessel operating out of the two ports. Often simply the generic term 'ship' is used, or even the archaic French word 'nef', but barges and balyngers are also often mentioned. Such descriptions appear, for example, in lists of ships licensed to carry pilgrims to Compostela in Spain during the first half of the fifteenth century.

In 1413 a 'nef', the St. Leonard of Weymouth, took 40 passengers there. In 1415 a balynger, also called the St. Leonard, probably the same ship, took 80. In 1428 the Holigost of Weymouth, a larger ship, probably a 'cog', took 120. In 1434 a 'ship' the St. Nicholas of Weymouth took 30. In 1445 a 'barge', the James of Weymouth, took 50. In 1455 a 'ship', again called the James of Weymouth and probably the same barge, took 30. Ships requisitioned for service in royal fleets also provide information. When, in 1442, an attempt was being made by Act of Parliament to create a navy by having 'upon the See continuelly for the sesons of the yere fro Candilmes to Martymess, viii shippes with forestages; ye which shippes as it is thought must have on with another eche of hem CL men', every ship was to have attending it a barge manned by 80 men and a balynger with 40. There were also to be an unspecified number of 'spynes' (pinnaces) with 25 men each. The only Dorset port contributing to this fleet was Weymouth where Henry Russel sent one barge and one balynger, a not insignificant contribution to a squadron planned to consist of 24 substantial vessels.

In these lists the largest type was the cog. Clinker built, it was broad-beamed and high-sided giving the hull a rounded shape. It was capable of carrying large cargoes and its high freeboard made it easy to adapt for war by adding 'castles' fore and aft and also a 'top castle'. It was rigged with a single mast midships and a square sail. From the twelfth century onwards cogs were the main cargo vessels in northern waters until they were replaced by more developed designs such as the carrack and caravel. Another northern type was the 'hulk'. The only depiction of a medieval ship which can definitely be associated with Melcombe, on the borough seal of c.1285, is probably one of these. It shows a number of the characteristics associated with this type - a banana-shaped hull, a single mast, a rudder on the larboard quarter and no end posts[51]. Balyngers and barges were oared ships which often also had masts. The name balynger derived from the fact that the type developed from whalers used by the Basques.. They ranged from 20 to 50 tons and possibly larger. They had a reputation for being fast and manoeuverable and were often used by pirates and privateers. Barges were similar to balyngers, but usually bigger. In wartime all these types were requisitioned for naval service, but as warships they could not compete with galleys[52].

On ship size, the rolls of the royal fleets provide the most comprehensive information. In the fourteenth and fifteenth centuries the four Dorset ports of Poole, Lyme, Weymouth and Melcombe were repeatedly required to provide ships for the king's service. Generally, they supplied roughly equivalent numbers, but there were occasions when comparatively greater burdens were placed on Weymouth and Melcombe. For example, in 1324 when war with France threatened, they were required to provide ten ships compared to Poole's four and Lyme's two. This levy furnishes detailed information about the sizes of the vessels involved. Weymouth sent two, each of 200 tons, together with one of 140 and one of 120; Melcombe sent one of 120 and one of 110. This compared with two from Poole of 160 tons and from Lyme one of 160 and one of 140. These were all quite large ships for their time with crew sizes ranging from 50 to 25[53].

Much has been made of the apparently disproportionate number of ships sent to the siege of Calais in 1346, when Weymouth (and Melcombe) sent either 15 ships and 264 men, or, according to other sources, 20 ships and the same number of men. This was many more than Poole's 4, Lyme's 4, Wareham's 3 and, more startlingly, not many fewer than Southampton's 21, Bristol's 22, London's 25 and Plymouth's 26. It has been pointed out, however, that in the Calais fleet roll, which refers to 83 ports, the ships enumerated are nearly all small ones. Large ships would have gone aground off Calais, so small coasters of light draught were required. The size of Weymouth's and Melcombe's contribution, therefore, may reflect the importance to them of the coasting trade[54].

Chapter 5

War, disease and decline

When John Leland paid his visit to Weymouth and Melcombe in the 1530's he was struck by how small the 'tounlets' were. Weymouth, he observed, was the larger; but Melcombe 'as yt ys evidently seene, hath beene far bygger than yt ys nowe', and the cause of Melcombe's decline, he was told, 'ys layd onto the Frenchmen, that yn tymes of warre rased thys towne for lak of defens'[55]. He did not go on to describe what he had seen, but it seems fairly clear that in the early decades of the sixteenth century both places were showing signs of decline and decay, Melcombe more so than Weymouth.

In some accounts the onset of this decline is ascribed to the outbreak of the 'Black Death' in 1348, almost two hundred years before Leland's visit, a view perhaps influenced by Melcombe's notoriety (whether deserved or not) as the port through which the disease had first entered England. Leland, however, judged differently and in forming his opinion he was undoubtedly picking up on stories which had been current in Melcombe for many years which put the blame on French attacks on the town in the later years of the fourteenth century. Neither of these simple beliefs is a sufficient explanation of decline in itself, however. Disease and war each made their impact on both towns in complex ways, but it was the manner of their conjunction which proved ruinous.

Opinion is divided on whether, in fact, the Black Death did first enter England through Melcombe. Other contenders for that doubtful honour have been advanced, including Bristol and Southampton. Different chroniclers tell different stories and none of them was a direct observer of the initial appearance of the disease. The case for Melcombe was made by Franciscan friars in King's

Lynn and the monks of Malmesbury Abbey in Wiltshire[56]. Bristol's advocates were based in the north of England while Southampton was favoured by Henry Knighton, an Augustinian canon writing in Leicester half a century later in the 1390's[57]. The probability is that, given the nature of the disease and how it spread, it entered through a number of ports at more or less the same time. Exactly when it arrived in Melcombe is also not known. The Franciscans believed that people were already dying there in late June while the Malmesbury monks thought that it did not arrive until early July. An even later date is suggested by a letter written by Ralph of Shrewsbury, Bishop of Bath and Wells, on the 17th. of August at Evercreech in Somerset less than fifty miles from Melcombe. In the letter he ordered his archdeacons to urge the clergy and laity under their control to take part in intercessionary processions, to pray devoutly and incessantly, to confess sins, recite psalms and perform works of charity which, he hoped, would prevent 'a catastrophic pestilence from the East [which] has arrived in a neighbouring kingdom' [France] from stretching 'its poisonous branches into this realm'[58].

The Franciscans believed that the plague was brought to Melcombe by two ships, one of them a Bristol vessel, on board which were sailors from Gascony who were infected with the disease, which had been rampant in Bordeaux. Once it had arrived it rapidly spread to the inhabitants of the town. Geoffrey le Baker, a cleric of Swinbrooke in Oxfordshire, a contemporary, described how he had been told that a 'Dorset seaport' and then its hinterland had been 'stripped of its inhabitants'[59].

Although there has been some controversy about the exact nature of the Black Death, it is now clear that the disease involved was bubonic plague, Yersinia Pestis. A reconstruction of the genome of medieval Y Pestis, based on DNA recovered from remains in a London plague cemetery shows little difference from similar analyses of modern cases of the disease. The fourteenth century outbreak appears to have been the first great pandemic of a particularly virulent type which spread very quickly. It took two forms, depending on the mode of infection, and their gruesome symptoms are well known. When it was transmitted by infected fleas the result was the emergence of dark swellings (buboes) in the lymph nodes, usually of the groin, armpits and neck, after which the bacilli invaded other major organs, especially the lungs and spleen. Death might not occur for several days and some people were even known to have recovered. This type was bubonic plague. Person-to-person transmission occurred through the inhalation of plague bacilli from droplets of the sputum of an already infected individual. This was followed by coughing, breathing difficulties and eventual heart failure. This was pneumonic plague, it was more deadly and accounted for the rapid spread of the disease.

The Black Death was a disaster on a national scale. It has been estimated that it wiped out between 40% and 50% of the population of England, but there were local variations in its impact. It seems from Geoffrey le Baker's testimony that many people died in Melcombe and that the disease moved quickly outwards from the town. One of the best sources for showing the levels of mortality are the 'Books of Institutions', church documents which record the appointment of clergy to vacant livings. These registers give an idea of the numbers and frequency of clergy deaths and the parishes where they occurred when the plague was at its height. In the whole of Dorset one hundred appointments were made between October 1348 and April 1349. During these seven months the number of appointments as a result of deaths of incumbents rose from 4 to 17 to 28 and then fell slowly back to 21 then 12 and 12 again and then to 6 in April. In the following four months from May to August the numbers were 9, 3, 11 and 5. Previous to the outbreak the average number of institutions had been one per month. In the worst seven months, therefore, the mortality rate amongst priests in Dorset appears to have increased by more than 1300% and it was not until the autumn of 1349 that the number of institutions returned to normal.

Appointments to parishes around Melcombe show how the plague spread locally. Within weeks, by September 1348, West Chickerell had received a new incumbent who had himself died and been replaced by March. In October there were new institutions to Warmwell, Wool and Holy Trinity Dorchester. Clergy deaths then accelerated rapidly. Bincombe received new incumbents in November and March and there were also changes in this period in Osmington (twice), Chalbury (twice), West Chaldon (twice), Owermoigne, Radipole, Winterborne Monkton, Winterborne Came, West Knighton and West Stafford. To the west, the abbot of Abbotsbury died, as did the vicar, and there were new appointments made in Portesham, Punchknowle, Litton Cheney, Compton Valence and Askerswell[60].

An impression of what life must have been like while the plague was raging is given by various chroniclers, although their accounts need to be treated with caution. First there was the terror caused by the approach of the disease, with people fleeing who could. Then they record the torment of its symptoms and the disgust at its aftermath with the sick and dying being abandoned by their families and the dead left unburied. Churchyards could not cope with the numbers of burials, so plague cemeteries were set up in fields where corpses were thrown into mass graves. Crops were left unharvested and stock unchecked, indeed many animals were dying from a simultaneous outbreak of murrain. While the general tone of the chronicles is one of sympathetic horror, some wrote disapprovingly about what they saw as the almost immediate social dislocation caused by the death rate. Henry Knighton thought that the 'humble' were humble no longer and were getting above themselves, with labourers and servants taking advantage of their scarcity value and demanding higher wages. In response to these efforts at wage-bargaining the crown issued the Ordinance of Labourers in 1349 which attempted to force people to accept offers of work whilst pegging wages. This was frequently ignored and recalcitrant workers were faced with imprisonment or taking to the woods. In Knighton's words, employers - 'abbots, priors, greater and lesser knights and others of both greater or lesser standing in the country' - who were anxious to get their crops harvested and work done , pandered to 'the arrogance and greed of the workers' by paying up and if they were caught were themselves fined for breaking the Ordinance. Even priests were demanding more, Knighton complained. Whereas before the plague a man could get a chaplain for four or five marks, or for two marks with board and lodging, no-one would now accept a vicarage at £20 other than 'ignorant' men whose wives had died and were rushing into holy orders.

All this disruption is often presented as the beginning of the breakup of those ties and obligations which for centuries had bound peasants to the lands of their manorial lords and to the dissolution of the 'system' of manorial economy. But the causes of this are much more complex than simply the outbreak of 1348, however devastating that was; although as the plague came back again and again in the 1360's and 1370's it did increase already existing pressures for change in that system. What happened in Melcombe in 1348 may not have been the cause of this profound revolution, but it was certainly a harbinger of it.

The Black Death decimated the populations of the towns of Weymouth and Melcombe themselves and their hinterlands, affecting their trade and drying up the supply of regenerating incomers. So far as the towns were concerned, this might not have taken many years to recover from. But while the consequences of plague were still being felt new disasters overtook them.

During the thirteenth, fourteenth and fifteenth centuries English kings fought many wars -against the Welsh and the Scots, but most of all against the French, as English and French monarchs struggled to retain or gain control of large parts of France. By the end of his reign in 1216 King John had lost many of the French possessions that English kings had amassed since 1066 - in Normandy, Maine, Anjou, Touraine, Poitou and Brittany. The English managed to hold onto Gascony in the south west but were generally unsuccessful in their attempts at recovery elsewhere. In 1337, however, King Edward III formally laid claim to the French throne and there began a long series of campaigns to regain the 'English' lands which has come to be known as the 'Hundred Years' War', although it lasted considerably longer than a century.

Weymouth and Melcombe were drawn into these dynastic conflicts because the Channel and the south coast of England became, in effect, a 'war zone'. This was inevitable since sea routes provided the only links between the lands of the English kings in both England and France. Also, through the Channel passed trade routes which were vital to the English economy. The French were bound to try to damage their enemy by disrupting these, the English to maintain them at all costs and to inflict similar damage on the French. The result was a confused mixture of raids by English and French squadrons on each others' coasts and shipping which went on for years. In fact, as Rodger makes clear, 'raiding, the deliberate destruction of resources, lay at the heart of medieval [naval] strategy'. He goes on to show that while it was difficult to intercept ships on the open seas, it was relatively easy to locate and destroy their home ports. Galleys were very effective for this and the results were equally ruinous for merchants and their trade.[61] The wars also provided many opportunities for individual privateering and outright piracy. In fact it was difficult for ship masters to know who were enemies and who were friends; because it was not only the French and their allies and mercenaries who attacked English shipping, English vessels preyed on each other as well as on the French. In fact the ships of the Cinque Ports were notorious for attacking other English shipping. In 1321, for example, they had assaulted Southampton and burned Portsmouth and in the same year King Edward II had to order the men of the Cinque Ports on the one hand and those of Poole, Lyme, Weymouth and Melcombe to cease from attacking, robbing and murdering each other and burning each others' ships. A year later Weymouth men robbed and scuttled a ship from Plymouth. As for the raids themselves, they were brutal and destructive and there was little that a medieval port such as Weymouth or Melcombe, with their small populations and inadequate defences could do against them. Nor was there help at hand. Men living within an area of a specified number of leagues from the coast, known as 'maritime land', were supposed to form a coastal militia under the command of a local lord. But, although in times of crisis a signalling system of clifftop beacons was organized, it was difficult to mobilise and deploy these forces. By the time they arrived at the ports, if they ever did, the raiders, who often used fast war-galleys were long gone,

All- out war began in 1337 with a French raid on Portsmouth, followed by a particularly devastating one on Southampton in 1338. Soon after this the French fleet was virtually destroyed at the great sea-battle of Sluys in 1340 when 190 out of the 213 French ships present were captured by the English. But the raids did not stop. In the same year the French admiral Robert Houdetot, with a squadron of three galleys, seven armed barges and some armed Spanish ships swept through the Channel capturing an English convoy of thirty vessels carrying wool and slaughtering their crews. They next laid waste the Isle of Wight and Portland[62].

The active role played by Weymouth and Melcombe in the early phases of these wars consisted mainly in supplying ships for the king's fleets, since at this time there was no organized standing royal navy. English kings owned some ships, but had to rely on requisitioning merchant vessels which were then re-equipped for war. The procedure, known as 'arresting', was that the crown sent out sergeants-at-arms who, in cooperation with town bailiffs, selected ships for service. They were then fitted out with fore-

and rear-castles and fighting tops if they were to operate as men-of-war, or alternatively they were equipped to transport troops, horses and supplies. Naval operations were risky and ship masters tried to dodge being arrested, a practice known as 'eloignment'; or, once their designated task was completed they tried to get back to their normal business as fast as possible. In 1342 King Edward III assembled an enormous fleet of 357 vessels for the transport of troops and supplies to Brittany, to which Weymouth and Melcombe contributed four ships. Weymouth possibly also contributed four barges to another fleet for the same expedition. Once they had unloaded, a number of ships deserted, including at least two from Weymouth, leaving the king in the lurch. When Edward returned from Brittany in 1343 he landed at Weymouth and presumably made his feelings clear. As is well known, soon afterwards in 1346/7 the two towns made their largest single contribution of either fifteen or twenty ships to the fleet gathered for the siege of Calais, although their sizes and the role they played is not recorded[63].

Throughout the wars direct damage was done to the shipping of Weymouth and Melcombe. Many vessels were destroyed. In 1375 a convoy of thirty nine ships, including three from Weymouth, was lost in Bourneuf Bay, on the Breton coast[64]. Impressment also caused financial damage by taking ships away from their trading activities especially since, as the wars dragged on, owners and crews were not being paid by the crown. The results of this can be seen in the dwindling contributions made by the towns. Weymouth provided two ships for a fleet in 1383, but by the beginning of the fifteenth century the towns' resources were so depleted that in 1401 Weymouth had to be grouped with Seaton and Sidmouth to provide a single balynger and Melcombe with Poole and Wareham to send a barge[65]. Weymouth provided one ship for Henry V's fleet in 1417 for the follow-up to the Agincourt campaign. After that the only identifiable contribution made by Weymouth was the selection in the 1440's of a barge and a pinnace belonging to Henry (or Harvey) Russell to take part in an elite squadron mobilised against privateers and pirates. Melcombe is no longer mentioned.

It was in the later decades of the fourteenth century, however, that the lasting material damage was done to the two ports themselves and especially to Melcombe. Accounts of raids on Melcombe and Weymouth refer particularly to the years 1377 and 1386. In 1377 King Edward III died and was succeeded by his ten year old grandson, Richard II. Perhaps taking advantage of this royal minority and also because more ships were becoming available to him as a result of the recent establishment of a royal shipyard in Rouen, the Clos des Gallees, King Charles V of France ordered the recommencement of large scale raiding on the south coast of England.

According to Froissart's chronicle on the 26th. June, five days after Edward's death, a French fleet under Admiral Sir John de Vienne and a Spanish Admiral, Sir Fernando Sausse, attacked the port of Rye *'which they burnt...and put to death the inhabitants, without sparing man or woman....After this exploit the French landed in the Isle of Wight. They afterwards burnt the following towns:Portsmouth, Dartmouth, Plymouth and several others. When they had pillaged and burnt all in the Isle of Wight, they embarked and put to sea, coasting the shores until they came to a port called Pog [Poole]....They burnt part of the town of Pog...embarked and coasted towards Southampton and attempted to land but were prevented from doing so....[They] then sailed [for] Dover and landed and attacked Lewes[66].'*

M. Oppenheim, writing the maritime history chapter in the Victoria County History of Dorset, maintained that this was the occasion of the first really devastating raid on Melcombe. He believed that Melcombe was one of the 'several others' mentioned which in 1377 were 'more or less wasted'. He cited 'one chronicler' as his source for this but does not name him. As further evidence Oppenheim also connected the attack to the beginning of petitions for relief from Melcombe in 1378[67].

In this Oppenheim appears to have been following the third edition of Hutchins' 'History' in which the editors, Skipp and Hodson, also linked this attack to the petitions. They had gone farther, however, and related how 'an old chronicler has left us this account of the destruction of Melcombe' and then quoted a well-known passage which purports to give a vivid description of the raid.

'The French kynge on his part greatly fortyfied hys navie that he hadde on the see, and kept the streightes between Engelond and France, they did great damage to the realm of England, ther was non that coude yssue out of England but they were robbed, slayne or taken, and one Sunday, they came in the forenoone, to the haven of Melkum, when the pepel were att masse, and the Normaynes, Genowaies, Bretons, Pycardes and Spanyerdes, entered into the towne and robbed and pylled the towne and slewe divers, and defowled maydens and enforced wyves, and charged their vessels with that pillage, and so entered agayne into their schyppes, and when the tide came they disancred and sayled to Normandie, and came to Depe, and their departed and devyded their boty and pyllages[68]*'.*

Skipp and Hodson took the account from George Alfred Ellis' 'History' of 1829. Ellis, however, related it not to 1377 but to a raid on Melcombe in 1386 at a time when the French King, Charles VI, had been assembling since 1383 a large army and invasion fleet in Sluys. Ellis wrote 'in 1386 the French collected a large fleet and army at Sluise, for the express purpose of invading England. King Richard made great preparations to repel them, but some of the flotilla escaped and upon this coast did an infinite degree of damage. Melcombe fell in for its share, for they landed from their fleet and laid waste the country with fire and sword, the houses were nearly all burned to the ground.[69]' Ellis then goes on to quote the passage above. Unfortunately, he also provided no reference for it whatever, not even attributing it to an 'old chronicler'.

The graphic and dramatic character of the passage and especially the language in which it is written have, over the years, lent credibility to it as a detailed, almost eyewitness, account of events which actually happened. Alas, this is not the case. Most of it is, in fact, a rehash of the Bourchier translation, published between 1523 and 1525, of a description in Froissart's Chronicle, not of a raid on 'Melkum' but of the attack on Southampton in 1338. This can be seen from the original 1523 text below.

'...and assone as Sir Hewe Quyriell, Sir Peter Bahuchet and Barbe Noyre: who lay and kept the streightes bytwene England and Fraunce with a great navy knewe yt the warre was opyn. They came on a Sonday in the fore noone to the havyn of Hampton whyle the people were at masse; and the Normayns, Pycardes and Spanyerdes entred into the towne and slewe dyvers and defowled maydens and enforced wyves; and charged their vessels with ye pyllage And so entred agayne into their shyppes and when the tyde came they dysancred & sayled to Normandy and came to Depe. And there departed and devyded their boty and pyllages'[70]

Even as an account of the wasting of Southampton this is hardly first hand since Froissart was aged one at the time and did not come to England until 1361 when he stayed for five years. He did not visit again until 1394.

There can be no doubt, however, that the towns were attacked, particularly Melcombe, but the main evidence for this is to be found in the series of petitions for relief to the king and parliament, especially in the reigns of Richard II and Henry IV, and inquisitions into the state of the town. In the late 1370's they asked for assistance to wall the town and for additional privileges to help their businesses similar to those of Southampton (which was still being affected by the raid of 1338) both of which were refused. In the 1380's and 1390's the Melcombe burgesses repeatedly petitioned for relief from taxation and for remission or abatement of the 'fee farm' which, they claimed, had become 'unbearable'. In this, as will be seen, they were usually successful.

As is common in such cases (many other ports were doing the same), the language of these petitions is overwrought and claims are exaggerated. A number of the Melcombe petitions also reiterate the problems and terms of preceding ones in order to strengthen their claims for relief. This practice creates a rather confusing impression of the sequence of events, but overall a dismal story emerges. From an unspecified time in the reign of Edward III when the town was said to be well built and occupied by one hundred and twenty prosperous burgesses and many rich merchants and when it had substantial mercantile and fishing fleets, things had clearly gone badly wrong. Primarily as a result of repeated wastings and burnings only twenty burgesses were said to have remained in the town by the 1390's ,who said they could no longer afford the 'unbearable' charges being laid on the town. King Richard II was evidently convinced of their plight because in 1389/90 he remitted the fee farm and the tax known as 'tenths' for a period of twelve years. Things continued to get worse, however, and more petitions, now complaining that the town was more or less completely abandoned, led in 1408 to King Henry IV appointing an Inquisition to look into its state. The Commissioners took evidence *'by the oath of good and lawful men of the county dwelling outside the town and not having lands or tenements within it'*, to avoid special pleading. They found that the town had been wasted in 1377 and repeatedly burned and destroyed later and that it was now so desolate and its inhabitants so poor that there were only eight burgesses and tenants there who were not enough to pay the yearly fee farm or the 'tenths' and so, they warned, unless they were given help *'they will have to leave it entirely and depart to dwell elsewhere to the great and heavy damage and prejudice of the king in the customs and subsidy of the port amounting to one thousand marks which he used to receive there.*[71]' Accordingly in 1410 Henry IV reduced their annual fee farm from eight marks to twenty shillings and their 'tenths' to six shillings and eight pence after yet another petition.

At about the same time c1409 the town suffered a natural disaster. The piers, along with ships and barges, had been destroyed in a violent storm which had also flooded the town so that the greatest part of it had to be vacated. So much damage had been done to the functioning of the port, it was claimed, that the town's income had dwindled to the product of the revenue from market tolls, the grist mill and the perquisites of the borough court. The petitioners tried to convey the consequences of this devastation and dereliction by once again pointing out that if nothing was done and the merchants continued to stay away (suggesting that overseas trade had virtually disappeared) then the king himself would indeed lose the annual one thousand marks in customs and subsidies.

The continuing weakness of Melcombe in the early decades of the fifteenth century eventually led to another petition in 1432; this time not from its own burgesses but from those of Poole who, with their mayor, asked that Melcombe's status as a port be annulled[72].

'To our soverayne Lord the King plese it to your Royall matie...[that] your porte of Melcombe [suffering from]...scarste of healpe of pepole to...resyst the ennemies...[whereas] your towene and havon of poole is well...manned and there ys a seway...haven...wheare yor mayor and burgesses ben fully purposed, yor gracyos lycens there to had, to walle incarnell and fortefey yor sayd towne.[wherefore the petitioners pray the King]...to annull the sayd porte of Melcombe..The commons ben assented to this byll'.

The Poole burgesses were successful in their campaign to usurp Melcombe's position as a customs port and in July 1433 an Act of Parliament transferred that status. The terms of the Act once again make clear what had happened to Melcombe.

'The Portes of Melcombe and Poole

To our soverain Lorde the Kynge.Plese it to your Rial Mageste, bi thavis of your discrete and noble Counseil having consideration to the feblesse and nonsufficeante of your Porte of Melcombe, nought

*enhabited, ne of strengthe to considere the Goodes and Marchaundises
of your Marchantz it usynge, as it seemed welle, by the losse that John
Roger and other hadde ther late, for lakke and scarcete of helpe of
peuple, to withstonde and resiste the malice of youre enemys, to grete
fere and doute to youre Marchantz to shippe eny goodes of value there,
the whyche is both hurtynge of your custume, and hyndrnge to your
seid Marchantz; and on the tother vside, gracious Liege Lorde, howe
your Toune and Havyn of Pole is wele enhabited and manned and
yere is is a seure and sufficeaunte Havene for shippes, where youre
Mair and Burgeys been fully purposed, your gracious licence thereto
hadde, to walle, enkernell and fortefie your seid Towne and Havyn
sufficiently, by Goddes grace, for the saufgarde of alle Marchaundises
and other Goodes thedir comynge: and also yn strengthynge and
encresinge of alle the Cuntre yeraboute. Whereuppon it like to youre
seid Mageste, to graunte hem youre seid licence, so to fortefie the seide
Towne and Havyn, and yn relevation of that charge of youre habunant
grace to annulle theseide Porte of Melcombe, and make youre seid
Towne and Haven of Pole a Porte: so that alle manere Marchantz,
bothe Denizeins and Straungers mowe ther have shyppinge, and
dyschargynge of alle manere Marchaundises, Stapleware and other,
as frely as yn any of youre Portes: and that youre Mair ther, may
have sufficeant power to take rccognisances of the Staple, and to
have and use all other Fraunchises and Libertees as the Porte of
Southampton hath, any Statut or Ordenance of the contrarie made
nouzt withstondinge; yn the wey of Charite.*[73']

An additional problem which had clearly influenced the
passing of the Act was that part of the receipts of the customs
and subsidies of Melcombe had been used to directly support
Sir John Radclyf, the King's Seneschal of the Duchy of Guienne,
and these were in arrears, further evidence of the town's poverty.
This responsibility was now also transferred to Poole. Melcombe
therefore reverted to the status of a 'creek', although Poole does not
seem to have made much of these advantages in the longer term.

In 1454, for example, Poole and Melcombe jointly were required to pay £50 towards maintaining a squadron at sea[74], implying that Poole had not profited much from its newly gained advantages over Melcombe; and William Camden, writing in the sixteenth century, observed laconically that Poole 'since Richard III by the sloth and idleness of the townsmen is decayed'[75].

Although Weymouth was attacked in 1377, it appears to have suffered much less directly from the wars than Melcombe. This is not simply a matter of lack of local evidence. There is no record in the national archives of Weymouth bombarding the crown with petitions for relief as is the case with Melcombe. It may be that Melcombe was a more tempting target, indicating that earlier it had been more prosperous than Weymouth. It was certainly more vulnerable to attack by ships simply running up onto the beach and disembarking attackers who could then easily strike into the town.

The effects of the wars were felt through much more than physical damage, however, and Weymouth, like Melcombe, was liable to the financial problems caused by the demands of the crown and the impressment of its ships for royal service. Equally important were the constant disruptions of trade and a collapse of the confidence of those merchants and visitors who had been used to operating out of the towns, with a resultant loss of revenue for them. In particular, Weymouth must have been affected by the dramatic reduction in the wine trade from as early as 1338. Nevertheless, it was Weymouth ships which played a significant role in conveying pilgrims to the shrine of St. James of Compostela in the first half of the fifteenth century and which continued to be requisitioned for royal fleets, which suggests that its trade had not suffered as much as that of Melcombe. In the longer term both ports were affected by the general decline of Anglo-French trade after the loss of Normandy and Gascony between 1449 and 1453. Hutchins suggested that the raising of Melcombe's fee farm to £20 in 1450 indicates a recovery, but it has been shown that

Melcombe particularly and to a lesser extent Weymouth were obtaining significant (in Melcombe's case massive) reductions in their assessment for lay subsidies from 1433 and that these were made at the behest of the crown[76]. By 1489 Henry VII was confirming arrangements made by Henry VI for once again lightening the town's burdens because of its poverty and returning the amount of the farm to 20 shillings. This was confirmed again by Henry VIII in 1512 in consideration of the fact that the *'town has long ago been spoiled by our enemies of France and Normandy to the impoverishment and manifest annihilation of the Burgesses and is likely to be left as desolate'* unless given some assistance[77]. This was the situation found by Leland some twenty years later.

Chapter 6

Religion

Until the very end of the thirteenth century there was no place in either Weymouth or Melcombe for worship or other religious observances. This was not unusual. Thirteenth century town foundations often did not incorporate a parish church from the outset. Melcombe was part of the parish of Radipole until 1606, when the first St. Mary's church was built, and Weymouth did not gain its own parish church until 1836, remaining part of the parish of Wyke Regis until that time. Providing churches with parochial status in either would have infringed the rights of their 'mother' parishes and encroached on the latters' income. As a result the granting of parish status to the two towns was opposed by both Radipole and Wyke and also by the diocese of Salisbury and, instead, each was conceded a 'chapel of ease' - buildings, not necessarily of any great consequence, where religious worship could take place.

In Melcombe a chapel, listed as 'ecclesia', is recorded in a document known as the 'Taxatio Ecclesiastica'[78] which was compiled between 1288 and 1291. This was a list of ecclesiastical benefices (livings) valued at more than six marks (£4) per annum and was made in connection with a grant to King Edward I by Pope Nicholas IV of one tenth of the ecclesiastical income of England and Wales to pay for a crusade. In other documents dated 1298 this chapel is described as having been 'lately built' and still unconsecrated[79]. The inhabitants of Melcombe were clearly becoming impatient with this situation as is shown by an incident in 1301 when two priests, perhaps encouraged by the townspeople, were reprimanded by Simon of Ghent, bishop of Salisbury, for 'intruding' in the chapel (i.e. taking services there)[80]. It is named as the chapel of St. Mary in deeds of the 1360s and 1390s.

There appears to have been a chapel on the Weymouth side by 1321 when it was the subject of a complaint by another bishop of Salisbury, Roger de Mortival, alleging that the Weymouth townspeople, by attending it, were damaging the interests of the parish of Wyke[81]. No such chapel was mentioned in the Taxatio of 1288/91, perhaps because the benefice was worth less than six marks. (A church in the list at 'Weybause' has been claimed to be this chapel[82] but this resulted from the misidentification of Weybause which in fact refers to Upwey). There are several references to a chapel of ease in Weymouth in ancient deeds between 1361 and 1393 and it appears to have been refounded or rebuilt in 1377 in a dominating position on top of the cliff overlooking the town. This chapel, dedicated to St. Nicholas, was approached from the town by a flight of steps leading from the High Street, later known as Chapelhay Steps; although the nineteenth century Weymouth historian, George Ellis, maintained that 'most every house in High Street had an ascent from their rear to St. Nicholas Street, so called from its leading to the chapel'[83].

From the end of the thirteenth century the townspeople of Melcombe made repeated attempts to gain parochial rights for their chapel which were equally repeatedly blocked by the authorities of Radipole parish and the Salisbury diocese. The concerns of the Radipole parish that such a concession would be an even greater drain on its income can be seen from the fact that the valuation of the 'ecclesia de Melecumbe' in the Taxatio at £6.13s.4d. already exceeded that of the 'ecclesia de Rappole' at £5. (In comparison the valuation of the 'ecclesia de Wyk' was £13.6s.8d.).

For the townspeople the problems caused by not having parish rights were both practical and spiritual. Baptisms, marriages and especially burials involved a long and burdensome trek to the parish churches at Radipole or Wyke. For those so minded things such as regular attendance at mass, the giving of oblations (offerings) and good works were a means of storing up spiritual credit; and, for those wealthy enough, paying to have masses and prayers said for dead relatives could diminish, they believed, the time to be spent by their souls suffering the fires of purgatory. For the parish priests, payments for spiritual services, mortuary fees and oblations represented income they were reluctant to forgo.

After this early evidence of anxiety to foster the religious life of the towns little is known about what progress was made for many years. Like everything else it must have suffered from the desolation caused by plague and war and it is interesting to speculate whether the possible rebuilding of the chapel of St. Nicholas in Weymouth in 1377 had anything to do with a possible raid on the town. In Melcombe there is no evidence concerning the chapel at this time, although it had not disappeared: in 1397 a certain John Shudde was brought before the borough court 'for placing dung in a vacant place opposite the chapel...to the grievous damage of the people walking there.'[84] However, in the second decade of the fifteenth century attempts to make better provision were renewed when in 1418 Dominican friars, or friars preachers as they were then generally known, were brought into the town, making Melcombe host to the last house of Black Friars to be established in England.

The initiative for this appears to have been taken by two lay persons, John Rogers of Bryanston and Hugh Deverell. They owned properties in Melcombe and Rogers was evidently a merchant there. He was the individual whose losses at Melcombe would be referred to some years later in the Act of 1433 when the town's 'port' status was transferred to Poole. It may have been that the introduction of friars was an attempt by the two men to reinvigorate the town by using friars as 'shock troops'. The Dominicans were well known for their educational, charitable and practical contributions to town life as well as for providing spiritual services, all of which they took out into the community. With the Dominicans the church came to the people rather than the other way round.

Deverell and Rogers approached the Provincial of the Dominican Order in England who applied to Pope Martin V for a licence to establish a friary in 1418. The Pope gave his permission to erect a convent for the Dominicans with a church, belfry, cloister and churchyard. This was going to be something altogether different from a chapel of ease. Deverell and Rogers supplied the land. This consisted of two 'messuages' with two 'tofts' and three 'curtilages' - i.e. two houses with associated yards amounting to a plot some 270 feet long by 160 feet broad.[85] It is clear that the early friars quickly got to work. The first prior, Edward Poldyng accompanied by friars John Lok and John Lowen, set up a temporary chapel and altar in one of the houses and began preaching. Almost as quickly they ran into opposition from John Chandler, bishop of Salisbury (1417-26). In 1425 he sent one of his court officials, the Commissary John Morton, to investigate the activities of the friars. Morton reported that they had erected an altar without the bishop's permission in a 'profane and inhonest place' and that many townspeople had helped them. The friars appear to have ignored the bishop and his commissary and carried on. The bishop then 'interdicted' them, excluding them from taking part in a wide range of sacraments, and denounced them for 'extorting' the 'oblations' and devotions of the townspeople who had come 'flocking to them' away from the parish church at Radipole. All religious celebrations were to stop and the friars and the people who had helped them were ordered to appear before the bishop in 1426. Chandler, however, died in that year[86].

Some time later, Rogers and Deverell, renewed their efforts to go ahead with the work. They firstly applied for a royal licence to continue with the building of the convent and obtained this in 1431. They and others in Melcombe then petitioned the new bishop, Robert Neville, for his permission also. After stressing the regularity of their proceedings and pointing out that they had both papal and royal licence, they then set out their motives for going ahead and their statement gives an interesting picture of the state of Melcombe at this time. They were moved to take action, they said, in a spirit of piety, because there was no place in Melcombe dedicated to God. (What had happened to the chapel of St. Mary by this time is not clear.) The parish church at Radipole, a mile and a half away was too distant and inconvenient for the townspeople, their families and others, including merchants coming to the town by land and sea. As a consequence of the lack of the services of clergy, the inhabitants of the town were 'extremely rough and ignorant' and the friars had been working hard for some time to overcome this. In addition, they were concerned about the desolation and poor physical condition of the town, situated as it was 'in angulo terrae' - ' in a corner of land'. Many places had been destroyed, the vill lay open to its enemies and, in consequence, the king's revenues from rents and customs were diminished (a point they had stressed in their application for a royal licence)[87]. The precise response of the bishop is not available but the interdict was removed and ordinations are known to have taken place in the friary church in 1434 and 1437.

The site of the convent was less than an acre and was bounded by present-day Maiden Street, St. Alban Street, Governor's Lane (earlier known as Friary Lane) and lay open to the beach on the east. This was land that had been occupied but was fairly marginal, as was often the case with friary sites in medieval towns. The church with its steeple and bell was built. Inside there was a marble altar in the choir and a number of side altars. The church lay in the southern part of the site with the all-important cemetery to the north. John Leland described it as a 'fare house of Freres yn ye este parte of ye Towne'.

The friary was the centre of the religious life of Melcombe for more than a century. Its attractions for the townspeople were primarily, of course, that it met what they thought to be their spiritual needs. They could regularly attend mass and confession and they could be buried in a place where masses and prayers were continuously being offered and where they could obtain such intercessions for dead relatives and for themselves after death. Accordingly, a cemetery was created on the north side of the friary where many skulls were dug up in 1682[88]. Even the disputes between the friars and the rectors of Radipole seem to have been eventually resolved. In 1533 Oliver Watson, Rector of Radipole and Portland, was buried in a tomb which he had built in the friary church and he was succeeded as Rector by Simon Ball, an ex-Prior of Melcombe. However, in 1538, in the reign of Henry VIII, all friaries were dissolved and the inhabitants of Melcombe were once again left without a place of worship until 1606.

Friars were popular in medieval towns. Besides their preaching and other spiritual services they often worked closely with the leading citizens of a town in more secular matters and this proved to be the case in Melcombe. During the 1440s they made a practical contribution to the restoration of the town by constructing a jetty to improve the harbour. One of the effects of this work, it has been claimed, was that it 'marked the first step in the movement of Melcombe harbour out of the Backwater and onto its present site'[89]. Later they decided to build a tower to make the town and port more defensible, as well as the friary itself. They applied to Parliament for assistance with this project and obtained a grant of a piece of land.1000 feet long and 600 feet broad, without rent, and also a sum of £10 per annum for twelve years from the customs and subsidies of the port of Poole towards the building costs. When, in 1450, as part of an economy drive, Parliament passed an Act of Resumption annulling all grants made by Henry VI, who was considered extravagant in this respect, the Melcombe friars were specifically excluded from its provisions

'in consideration of the grete charge and costes yat yey have hadde, and yet must have, in makyng and repairing of a Getey, in defensing of the said Towne of Melcombe ayenst the flowyng of the see'

An impression of the size and location of this jetty can be gained from two early maps: the 'bird's-eye view of the Dorset coast' of 1539 already mentioned and also a late sixteenth century plan of Portland, Melcombe and Weymouth attributed to Robert Adams[90]. From these can be seen the value of the jetty 'against the flowing of the sea', presumably preventing the deposition of sand by increasing the scouring effect of the tide, and the utility of the tower in the case of would-be assailants running their boats up onto the beach. The maps make clear also why Rogers and Deverell made such a thing about Melcombe's situation 'in angulo terrae'. In the event of a raid, once the neck of land to the north of the town, known as 'the Narrows', was blocked the inhabitants had nowhere to go; they were literally 'cornered'. After the 1440's some of them at least might hope to find refuge in the friars' tower.

Whether the people of Weymouth availed themselves of the ministrations of the Dominicans is not known, nor whether the friars preached on the south side of the harbour. But, just as in Melcombe, it was also felt necessary to do something to mitigate the paucity of religious provision in Weymouth. One response to this by some burgesses was to create a religious fraternity, a development that was happening at this time in many towns. In 1442 Henry VI licensed Adam Moleyns, Dean of Salisbury, and others in the parish of Wyke (i.e. Weymouth townspeople) to found a fraternity or guild in the chapel of St. Nicholas in the borough of Weymouth. Its title was to be 'The Mayor and Wardens of the Fraternity or Guild of St. George of Weymouth'[91]. As such it fulfilled more than simply religious functions, giving prominent citizens opportunities to hold office and to wield influence in the town.

Mainly, however, such fraternities were devoted to religious and charitable activities. One of their characteristics was the carrying out of elaborate processions, especially on Corpus Christi day (which fell variably between 21st May and 24th June). This was the case with the Weymouth fraternity, as the following extract from its licence indicates.

'None shall fail at the setting forth of the procession on Corpus Christi day, on pain of forfeiting one pound of wax, and each brother shall pay six pennies to the procession and shall pay yearly'.[92]

The wax was mainly for candles, of which one might be kept burning permanently at the fraternity's altar in the chapel, or for use during a special mass, when many might be required. Processions themselves were an important aspect of the religious life of a town. The payment of six pennies for the procession gives an indication of the status of the brothers.

Also associated with the Fraternity was a Chantry. It too was endowed in the 1440s by Henry Russell, the Weymouth shipowner. He provided it with seventeen 'messuages' (properties) and twenty eight acres of land in Weymouth, Knighton, Wooton, Glanville, Portland and Wyke. Later, in the 1450s, Russell appears to have made additional grants bringing the total land in the endowment to fifty four acres with common for eight oxen. The first chantry priest was John Longman who came from a chapel in Canterbury, presumably a background which was considered to attest to his suitability[93].

The specific purpose of a chantry was to say masses for the souls of the dead, which were popularly believed to count against time to be spent in purgatory. Usually these were for the benefit of the endower and his family, but also other people joined religious fraternities, such as that of St. George, to cooperate in having masses said for the members. Their names would be entered on the 'bede roll' - a list of names of beneficiaries which would be read out on Sundays and at Christmas and Michaelmas by the priest or the 'bedeman'. In 1455 the value of this endowment was £6. 13s. 10d. When the chantries were suppressed in 1547 its value was £6. 14s. 10d. which at the time was about the usual stipend to support a chantry priest.

When the chantry was dissolved the Weymouth burgesses complained that once again they were being deprived of religious provision. A memorandum in the chantry roll tells a familiar tale.

"The Inhabts of Weymouth above said saieth that the said towne of Weymouth is distant from the Parishe Church in Wike a myle and more and that ther is nowe other chapell in the church of the said Towne but onely the said Chapell of St George and that the said Towne of Weymouth is a Haven Towne and lieth veray daungerous for enemyes to envade the same so that if the said chapell or living of the priest to serve in the same should be denied and that the Inhabitants sholde be enforced to go so farre to ther parish church in Wyke enemies in thabsence of the Inhabitants of Weymouth might invade the same to the greate losse and hinderaunce as in the certificat exhibited to the Kings Commissioners amongst other"[94].

As has already been suggested, religious fraternities often had multiple aims, some not explicitly spiritual. The other agenda of the Mayor and Wardens of the Fraternity of St. George was to set Weymouth free from all vestiges of the tutelage of the parish of Wyke. This was not to be achieved for another three hundred years. But Weymouth managed to retain its chapel when all the chantries were suppressed and their property sold off. A note appended to the Commissioners' memorandum by the future Elizabethan statesmen William Cecil read as follows

'Sir Frauncis Russell Knte by his father the L prevye Seale hath obteyned the preferment of the premises of my L Grace and yet he gentillie offereth to let the Chapell remayne to thuse of the Towne hereof. I thaughte to make you prevye W. Cicell.[95]'

Chapter 7

Town life in the fourteenth century

At the turn of the fourteenth century the records of borough courts held in Melcombe give a vivid picture of the everyday life of the town.[96] Although the documents that have survived cover only a few years between 1396 and 1400 with a few later ones from 1455 and 1456, the court's proceedings show the town government being set up for the year, while the details of cases which came before it give glimpses of the doings of ordinary people.

The records of two 'annual general meetings' of the court in September 1397 and September 1400 describe the election of officers for each of the following years. At these meetings a 'jury' of twelve burgesses chose the mayor, two bailiffs, two under-bailiffs, two constables and two 'collectors of the king's rents'. How the jurors themselves were elected does not appear, but they were obviously prototypes of councillors. The range of duties of these officers is not given, but the histories of similar towns suggest that they were very wide. The mayor, besides being the ceremonial leader of the town, presided over the courts and controlled the markets, while the bailiffs and constables carried out the court's orders. The mayor and bailiffs also represented the borough to the outside world, at the sessions and the county court in Dorchester, as petitioners to the crown and also (but not exclusively) at parliaments. In Melcombe the main preoccupation of the court was with the regulation of traders in the town by enforcing both the town's own ordinances and also the provisions of the national 'assizes' of bread and ale. It also dealt with town business concerning rents, debts and the maintenance of the 'Commonalty's' services.

The chief role of the constables was to maintain the peace and to police nuisances, of which there were many. Together with the mayor and bailiffs they were also responsible for keeping the town secure. This was done through the 'watch and ward' system of night and day patrols in which all male citizens had to do a stint or answer to the court if they defaulted. They could also raise 'hue and cry', which was principally a procedure for the pursuit and apprehension of felons but seems also to have been applied in Melcombe to errant animals.

One of the most noteworthy features of these two court meetings concerns the actual personnel who provided the town's governance. In each of these sittings, which were three years apart, the same individuals were elected to some of the posts. Thus, in both 1397 and 1400, Henry Forde became mayor, Eustace Kemer was one of the bailiffs and Roger Fox and Hugh Deer were under-bailiffs. Also at this time Thomas Cole is known to have been mayor twice, in 1396/7 and 1408/9, and in addition he held the office of collector of customs. Yet again the same names appear in the lists of members of parliament for the borough. Henry Forde went three times to parliaments at Westminster between 1378 and 1398. William Hellier, who was chosen as constable and one of the collectors of the king's rents in 1397, went three times to Westminster and once to Coventry between 1395 and 1414. Eustace Kemer and Thomas Cole went to Westminster in 1399/1400 and to the Gloucester parliament of 1407/8[97]. These two, therefore, must have been the members who presented the petition which led to King Henry IV appointing the Inquisition of 1408 into the state of the town, which produced the dire description of its circumstances which has already been mentioned.

What is clear from the recurrence of the same names in these documents is that the government of Melcombe was an oligarchy in the hands of a small, long-serving elite at the top of which were substantial merchants like Forde and Cole and another mayor of that time, John Abbot. All three traded in both wine and cloth, the businesses in which Melcombe fortunes were made. The bailiffs and constables were also members of this ruling group and evidence from the proceedings of the courts suggests that relations between them were not always harmonious. Factional rivalries existed leading to attempts to manipulate the court and sometimes descending into fisticuffs.

A fuller picture of the role of the bailiffs can be gleaned from the record of their expenses. In 1395 bailiffs William Hellier and Robert Calche were paid 13s. 4d.each for 'going to parliament [at Westminster] for the commonalty of the town'. During the year 1394-5 a total of 18s. 9d. was paid to the bailiffs for going to the sessions and county court 'holden in Dorchestre divers times'. This amount also included the expenses of the Steward for 'coming here divers times'. The Steward was the crown's representative, usually a lawyer, who looked after its interests in the borough. He was also paid wages of 40d. for the year. Expenses of 5s. 2d. 'all in' were paid to Sir Walter Clopton, Chief Justice of the King's Bench, 'when he came here'. The town also spent 2s. 6d. on 'fowls bought as a present' for Clopton. He was a long-serving lawyer who probably originated from Clapton, near Crewkerne, and who may have had family connections in Melcombe. Another Walter Clopton represented Melcombe in parliament in 1374. On the receipts side of the accounts bailiffs Kemer and Hellier delivered up the sum of 72s. 7½d. to the mayor, Thomas Cole, in 1396. This was almost certainly the product of rents.

The bailiffs were also responsible for managing the functions of the port. Money was spent on the town crane on the quayside. A cord bought for 'drawing up wine' cost 2s. 8d. and bonds of iron bought for the 'pollee' cost 8d. At the September 1397 court the jurors chose a certain Henry Clere and Hugh Deer, the under-bailiff, to 'keep a certain polye with a cord, belonging to the Commonalty of the ...vill and collect the profits thereof'.

They also looked after other aspects of town business. At a May meeting in 1397 Robert Walkelayn had undertaken that 'he will, before the feast of the Nativity next to come, erect a good and competent house for making a mill therein, in Melcombe Regis' and six sureties were found for him.

Actions for the recovery of debts frequently came before the court and its standard procedure was to 'arrest' - i.e. confiscate - goods as a surety for, or in lieu of, payment. Thus, the bailiffs 'arrested' two trees which were lying felled in the tenement of William Fyssher who owed ten years of rent arrears on his burgage. In another case two leaden' cuves', or measuring vessels, and other goods worth 40s. were arrested from the house of Walter Clopton for debt, but a certain John Swan broke the arrest by taking them away again. In yet another an individual whose name has been obliterated on the document was attached for debt by 'the arrest of a third part of 30 tuns of red wine'. This indicates a substantial debt owed by someone dealing in wine and also that significant quantities of wine were passing through the port.

In a town like Melcombe, then as now, many trades would have had to do with food and drink, both for sale in the town itself and for the victualling of ships. Ale was a particularly important commodity and a universal drink in an age without tea or coffee and when wine was expensive and the water suspect. Made and sold in ale-houses, it was also brewed domestically by 'ale-wives' or 'brewsters' who sold their surplus. It tended to go sour quickly and so its quality was regularly checked by ale-tasters (another role of the bailiffs). Its quality and price was regulated nationally by a statute known as the 'assize of ale' (as was bread) and it was also subject to local ordinances about quality and measures. As a result many cases coming before the court concerned breaches of the assize and the giving of short measure, reflecting the fact that, while the town authorities considered regulation to be very necessary, enforcing it was difficult. John Shudde, who was probably an ale-house keeper, was 'amerced' (fined) by the court for using an unfair quart measure. Ironically, it was because Shudde had made a plea of debt against Walter Clopton that the measuring vessels had been arrested from the Clopton housein the first place. Later Shudde appeared before the court to face a complaint that he had 'broken the arrest' of a cask of ale which had been seized by the ale-tasters who had declared that it was 'bad, not good and sound for the body of man'. In another case Edith Ketys was fined 3d. along with five others for breaking the assize with regard to brewing and also for using 'cups and other false measures'. Still others were fined for selling ale in vessels 'without the seal' and for unsupervised tapping (i.e. before the ale had been tasted). Under the terms of the assize repeat offenders were supposed to end up in the pillory or, in the case of women, on the 'tumbrell, trebuchet or castigatorie' - all colourful names for the ducking stool. In Melcombe the usual penalty seems to have been a fine which the brewsters paid up and then carried on as usual.

The fourteenth century, with its recurrent wars, has the reputation of having been a violent age and south coast towns, perhaps because of the frequency of seaborne raids, are known to have been more accustomed to violence than most. This again shows up in Melcombe's regular petitions for assistance. Many cases which came before the borough court, therefore, concerned offences 'against the king's peace'. Really serious crimes, or 'felonies', such as murder, arson or robbery were not prosecuted in the Melcombe court. In these cases the felon, if apprehended, was held in gaol until one of the king's justices came to hold a court of gaol delivery. The offences which were tried in the borough were mostly of the fist-fight type, but a variety of weapons was also used. For example, Thomas Sterer was charged with drawing a staff upon Agnes Capper and his wife, Cristina, with drawing a rake against Edith Ketes (the brewster). William Walkelyn (the miller) denied assaulting William Hellier with 'a certain stone', while the bailiffs accused Hellier of raising a club against Eustace Kymer, Henry Barbere and William Walkelyn, 'whether justly or not, they knew not'.

In a significant number of cases, however, daggers and swords were drawn, suggesting that weapons were carried routinely and more serious offences were committed. William Tilie drew a 'daggar' upon John Cokeman. Tilie was fined 3d. and his 'daggar' was confiscated, but then sold back to him for 8d. - a good example of how the court was used to generate income for the town. In a number of cases which involved the use of daggers and a 'baselard' (a cutlass) the bailiffs and under-bailiffs themselves were fined for failing to produce the weapons in court or for actually concealing them. Corruption was rife in the judicial system and the Melcombe court was no exception.

Fourteenth century towns were also dirty places. For example, the lack of organized procedures for disposing of butchers' and fishermen's/fishmongers' waste, or the effluent from trades such as tanning and dyeing, caused particular problems, as did the effects in the streets of having a large horse population. Domestic dunghills and cesspits in backyards were noxious and would also have to be cleared sooner or later. Dealing with nuisances was therefore a constant preoccupation of the court. Dung was frequently simply dumped in the streets. Maiden Street seemed to be favoured in this respect, although nowhere was safe. John Shudde (whose name often appears in these records on the wrong side of the authorities) was brought before the court 'for placing dung in a vacant place opposite the chapel...to the grievous damage of the people walking there'. Philip Attewell, Richard Kete, Edith Cartere and Thomas Russell were accused of placing dung on the quay at the eastern end of Russell's tenement 'to the nuisance of the whole vill'. Another kind of nuisance was obstructing the highway. Philip Bat was fined for putting a step on it near the door of his tenement.

Other incidents show the bailiffs dealing with the most detailed matters. A runaway horse had come into town 'from strange parts'.

The bailiffs had 'made cry' - i.e. had publicized its existence - but no-one had claimed it and so it was impounded. A different kind of lost property was a barrel of 'pych' which under-bailiff Roger Fox had found and brought to the notice of the court. When it was not claimed he made a 'fine' (i.e. completed a transaction) of 2s. for it with the court - another source of revenue.

Half a century later what little evidence there is suggests that the business of the court had not changed. In the very brief records of the proceedings of sessions held in 1455 and 1456 there are the perennial complaints of unpaid debts and rent arrears and the incorrigible breaches of the assize of ale. The court also kept an eye on dangerous dogs. At one hearing Robert Chapman was told that he had to remove a dog that was attacking and killing the poultry of his neighbours. At the next he produced witnesses to testify that his dog had not killed even a single goose. Peacekeeping was also kept up to scratch. In 1456 John Rogger had to answer to the mayor for not 'keeping his watch' by failing to turn up to do night patrols (he also owed five years' rent).

What all this shows is that life in fourteenth and fifteenth century Melcombe was pretty comprehensively regulated by the town authorities. Trades were controlled, individuals were chased up for causing nuisances, or blocking the streets, or keeping dangerous dogs, or not carrying out their civic duties. This level of (at least attempted) control was apparently common in many medieval towns where, unlike today, coercion was the only instrument available to them. How effective it was is another matter. In Melcombe these records also reveal that the authority of the constables was flouted, 'arrests' were broken, ale-tasters disregarded, bailiffs beaten up and the court itself sometimes manipulated, or disobeyed, or simply ignored.

Another type of court that was held in Melcombe at this time was known as a 'piepowder court' and there are records of sessions held in 1397 and 1398. Piepowder courts were held specifically to regulate markets or fairs. They settled disputes, enforced regulations of weights and measures and dealt with thefts and minor disturbances. Their purpose was to dispense speedy, summary justice before traders and visitors to the market had to (or took the opportunity to) leave town and they did this by giving decisions 'before the third tide' - i.e. within a day and a half.

The term .piepowder' derives from the French 'pieds poudrés', that is 'dusty feet'. It is commonly believed that the dusty feet belonged to people travelling in to the market; but an alternative view is that they were the feet of court officials who patrolled the site. The proceedings of the 1397 court were concerned entirely with public order offences: minor assaults, fist fights, hitting people with stones, making threatening gestures with clubs and the like. All were dealt with by either a bailiff or a constable, so the officers of the court obviously did act as market police.

Since 1314 Melcombe had had a market on Mondays. On market days the population in the town would swell as people from the surrounding area came in to sell their produce and buy domestic necessities. The area served by Melcombe's weekly market must have been quite limited, most probably to settlements south of the Ridgeway and east of the River Wey, although there would have been some overlap with Weymouth's catchment to the west (Weymouth's market day was Thursday). The great thirteenth century jurist Henry Bracton reasoned that the area served by a market would be limited by the time required for most people to get into town, carry out their business and return home. On that basis he recommended that markets should be no more than 6 miles apart. As has already been mentioned, however, the 1408 Inquisition into the state of the town claimed that Melcombe served a much wider area and that 'dwellers in the counties of Dorset, Somerset and Wiltshire...used to have their victuals and other necessaries in the town'. This would hardly have applied to the everyday contents of the weekly market and was probably a reference to the wider trade of the port. The Melcombe fair was a different matter. Granted in 1318 it stretched over the 'vigil, feast and morrow of St. Botolph the Abbot and the following five days' - i.e. the eight days between the 16th and 23rd June. People attending this would have travelled much longer distances and the range of goods would have been much wider[98]. John Hutchins, writing in the 18th century, recorded a tradition of a fair 'to which merchandize was brought from St. Malo, Cherburgh, Morlaix and other places in France'[99].

One further feature of these court records is worthy of note because it casts a somewhat different light on the succession of petitions for relief from the fee farm and tenths in the reigns of Richard II and Henry IV. As has been shown, these claimed that only 20 burgesses remained in the town in the 1390s and that this number had fallen to only 8 burgesses and 21 poor tenants *'dwelling in the vill'* in the early 1400s. However, using the court records it is possible to compile a list of 48 named individuals (who presumably had families) who were active in the town at this time. In addition, at a court held in May 1397 18 people were amerced for non-attendance. These included such personages as the abbots of Milton, Netley and Abbotsbury as well as the 'Lady of Beaumont'. At the September court in the same year 16 burgesses made default in appearing and were each fined 3d. Once again the abbot of Netley was included in the list and also this time the 'Lady of Frampton'.

The reasons for defaulting are not given, but the borough was clearly having problems with collecting and maintaining its rent income. A number of monastic institutions are known to have owned burgages in Melcombe. Some of these properties were probably used as cellars or warehouses by the abbeys. But monasteries were also absentee landlords who had bought up tenements and plots in towns to develop their own rent income and, as was happening in many other towns at this time, rents were shrinking. The court records also show that some Melcombe burgesses owed substantial arrears of rent. Melcombe was by no means unique in suffering from long-term decline, although in the early 1400s it had also gone through a severe crisis. However, it is clear that it had not been virtually depopulated and made derelict as the multiple petitions seem to suggest. There were still prosperous merchants in the town such as the Fordes, the Coles, the Abbots and others. When the Act of Parliament of 1433 transferred port status to Poole it named John Rogers, Walter Tracy and William Abbot as merchants who had sustained 'great losses' in Melcombe - but they had not abandoned the town.

What lay behind the petitions was a sustained effort to get the town's fee farm and tax liability reduced in times of difficulty. These were seen as additional burdens which were driving people away and making life harder for those who remained. Many other towns were carrying on similar campaigns and were, like Melcombe, making the worst of their situation in their petitions in the hope of securing relief.[100] However, the overall impression created by the court records is that, behind this facade, the town was 'carrying on' as far as possible with its usual business. Its administration was functioning and it seemed to have no difficulty in finding officers to fill the roles of bailiffs and constables. The markets were running. The port was being maintained to some degree. A new building was being proposed for the grist mill. Despite the self-interested claims of the mayor and burgesses of Poole in the 1430s, Melcombe may have been down, but it certainly was not out.

Chapter 8

The End of the Middle Ages

The question of when Weymouth can be said to have emerged from the 'middle ages' is not merely a matter of arbitrary dates; it has real meaning and raises many issues. How long, for example, did the towns' later medieval decline extend into the sixteenth century? What conditions needed to be present before Weymouth could be considered a 'modern' town? Clearly the centuries-long rivalry between the two old boroughs had to be resolved. Since this was based mostly on the sense of grievance of the inhabitants of Weymouth, who believed that somehow control of the harbour and its profits had been filched from them by Melcombe and that their ancient liberties were being subverted, its ending depended on the creation of a unified governance which alone could resolve these issues. Equally clearly, the extinction of the sense of separateness required the provision of a physical link between the two. As it turned out, both of these things were to prove difficult.

John Hutchins, believed that by 1450 Melcombe 'seems to have recovered its prosperity'. His evidence for saying this came from the Rolls of Parliament in which there is an order in that year directing that the fee farm of £20 (an increase) paid by the burgesses of the vill should be applied to the expenses of the King's household. This may have been more a reflection of Henry VI's urgent demands for money at a time when the costs of his household far exceeded his 'livelihood', than a sign of an improvement in Melcombe's situation which justified such an increase. For their part, whatever the reason for the increase, the Melcombe burgesses saw no reason not to stick to their long-term strategy of getting the fee farm reduced by continuing to plead poverty and 'spoliation'. In this they were once more successful and in 1489 a charter of Henry VII confirmed that the fee farm was once again 20s. and this was subsequently repeated by Henry VIII in 1512[101].

In fact, if one is trying to gauge how serious and long-standing the decline of the two towns had been since some supposed 'heyday' in the first half of the fourteenth century, the ups and downs of the Melcombe fee farm have little to offer. In order to make a more realistic assessment, some view has to be taken of three key dimensions: population, wealth and trade and physical development - i.e. by the early sixteenth century, were they more populous, were they richer, had they expanded? Fortunately, at this date, there is some evidence which makes possible at least an approach to these questions.

Although it is notoriously difficult to estimate population numbers, three sets of documents - the lay subsidy returns (taxation records) of 1525 and 1542[102] and the muster roll (militia list) of 1542[103] - suggest that for most of the first half of the sixteenth century the combined population of both towns cannot have been much greater than 400. As will be obvious from column 2 of the following table, if one is seeking to extrapolate total population numbers from them, the raw figures extracted from these documents present a number of technical problems in addition to the issue of the general reliability of such material. In the case of the lay subsidies, multipliers have to be devised to take into account evasion, exemptions (of the poor) and the fact that the tax was levied mainly on goods; in that of the muster roll to account for the fact that only able-bodied men aged between sixteen and sixty were listed; and, with both types of list to allow for the inclusion of females and other family members. For the purpose of drawing up this table a multiplier of 6.5 has been used for the lay subsidies and one of 3.75 for the muster roll.

Document	Number assessed or listed	Population
1525 lay subsidy	Weymouth 40	260
	Melcombe 25	163
Total population 1525		423
1542 lay subsidy	Weymouth 42	273
	Melcombe 22	143
Total population 1542		416
1542 muster roll	Weymouth 70	245
	Melcombe 43	151
Total population 1542		396

As can be seen from column 3 the resultant population figures are reasonably consistent and accord with Leland's observation in 1538 of the relative sizes of the two towns and the extreme smallness of both, implied as has been shown already by his coining of the term 'tounlet' to describe them. It should be remembered, however, as later surveys showed, that there would also have been a significant transient population in the towns at any given date.

As far as the wealth of the towns is concerned Leland also speaks of continuing decline - in the case of Melcombe at least - from a period of earlier prosperity. In trying to assess the scale of decline in wealth, a comparison is often made in the histories of other medieval towns between the lay subsidy of 1332 and that of 1525. With Weymouth and Melcombe, however, not much can be made of whether their gross wealth had decreased or not over that period. Nevertheless, what does emerge from such a comparison is that at both dates there was a similar pattern in the distribution of wealth in both places, in that they were each dominated by a small number of wealthy individuals. The prominence of the Shoydons, the Langynows and the Welyfeds in 1332 has already been discussed. In 1525 in Weymouth a similar pattern can be observed. Three men owned 44% of the assessed goods of which a certain Robert Samwise accounted for nearly 24%. In Melcombe the situation was even more extreme. One individual, John Raynolde, owned almost 78%. But not even Raynolde had the dominating status which Shoydon had relative to the rest of the county in 1332. Another interesting feature of the 1525 assessment is the substantial number of aliens in the ports - described as 'Normans' in the margins of the document. In Weymouth they amounted to 25% of those assessed and in Melcombe to a startling 40%, indicating the importance of the cross-Channel trade to the two ports[104].

If one is looking for signs of a recovery in the trade of the town, then the sixteenth century evidence is fragmentary and sometimes contradictory. There are some indications that the number of ships based in the port was increasing. In 1582, at a time of invasion threats from Spain, a survey of shipping returned that there were twenty ships and other vessels at the united borough of Weymouth and Melcombe. Three were of 120-150 tons and seventeen of 14-60 tons. Another survey made for the crown some forty years later in 1628 'of all the shipps, barques and vessels...with the muster of all the marriners, saylers and ffishermen' in the Dorset ports gives a total number of seamen for Weymouth as 176 and for Melcombe as 111 (the total of 287 being roughly a quarter of all the seamen listed for Dorset). The same document listed twenty six ships as belonging to the port, thirteen being at sea and thirteen at home. This compared with twenty ships from Poole and eighteen from Lyme. All except three of the Weymouth ships were under 100 tons, the average of the remaining twenty three being about 49[105].

Thomas Gerard, writing in the 1620s, took an optimistic view of the town's trade and economy claiming that the inhabitants 'gaine well by Traffique into Newfoundland where they have had 80 saile of Shippes and Barkes; as also by a nearer Cut into France opposite unto them, whence they return laden with Wines, Cloth and divers other usefull Commodities with which they furnish the Countrie'[106]. A port book of 1625 shows a flourishing trade with French ports, with 54 outward sailings and 52 inward as well as a significant trade with Irish ports[107]. It records only 1 inward sailing from Newfoundland in that year, however. This may have been due to special circumstances. For example, in 1622 the mayor had complained that the depredations of Algerine pirates had reduced the number of sailings to Newfoundland from 39 to 11[108].

At roughly the same time, the customs receipts from Weymouth in the second decade of the seventeenth century compared unfavourably with some other south western ports such as Exeter and Lyme (although in 1622 Weymouth was exporting more cloth and importing more wine than either Lyme or Poole)[109]. In 1628 a petition to the Duke of Buckingham described Melcombe and Weymouth as 'much decayed, for they and the town of Dorchester yielded the King £5000 p.a. in customs'[110].

With regard to the topography of the towns, in the later middle ages the shape and extent of both had changed little. Even by the mid-sixteenth century neither had expanded very far beyond those limits which historical geographers have termed 'fixation lines' - i.e. 'those demarkation lines denoting the margins of growth'[111]. In Weymouth these limits were the quayside and the steeply rising ground to the south; in Melcombe the quayside, the Backwater, the beach and the town ditch. As has already been shown, these features had effectively determined the physical characteristics of the towns over a long period.

Weinstock and Sellman's analysis of Elizabethan 'feoffments' (property conveyances) in Melcombe Regis suggests that little development had taken place beyond St. Alban Street before the 1550s.[112] The history of that part of the town known as the 'coneygar' bears this out. The coneygar had been important to Melcombe throughout the middle ages. A document of 1392 refers to 'the King's warren at Melcombe'[113] which would then have been a significant element in the town's economy. Coneys (only their young were called rabbits) were a valuable commodity and were prized both as a source of fresh meat (especially in winter) and also of fur which was used in lining and trimming garments and also for making hats. Because the animals were valuable and subject to extensive poaching attempts were made to confine them within warrens under the supervision and protection of a warrener. The boundaries of a warren were usually marked out by banks and ditches which were also attempts to keep the coneys inside. A late sixteenth century map of Weymouth and Portland, which has been attributed to Robert Adam,[114] shows another feature of the warren in the shape of a series of three low, flat-topped hillocks running across the northern end of Melcombe. These are named on the map as 'Coneybery Hills' and were obviously 'pillow mounds' – i.e. raised banks of earth which contained artificially created burrows. The reference to coneys is obvious and the 'bery' element derives from the fact that such mounds were often called 'buries'. The making of such features seems to have been especially prevalent in the sixteenth century, although there are plenty of medieval versions and it is impossible to say when the Melcombe ones were created...

Until towards the end of the sixteenth century there had been little encroachment into this part of the town. In 1563 Owen Raynolds, a member of an established Melcombe family and four times mayor, leased ' all that theyre conynger and warren of conyes ... as well within the said town as without' - i.e. on both sides of the town ditch - for a term of 21 years at 40 shillings per annum. The conditions of this lease make clear the undeveloped nature of the land involved. The 'highways and paths...tharbaige [herbage] and pasture' were reserved. He was forbidden to 'ordeigne any trenche, pale, hedge, dike or wall or other engyne'. The lease required him to replenish the warren yearly and allowed him only to erect a small house of 21x12 feet for 'the more savegarde of his said coneys' and to set traps for cats, dogs and other 'vermyne'. Sixteen years later this area was much the same. In 1579 Barnarde Maior took over the lease of ' all that there conigeare…called Melcombe conigeare on the north side of the Towne ditch' for a further 22 years at the same rent and in addition he had to furnish forty couple of coneys and leave at least one hundred couple in the warren. He, too, had to meet additional requirements, including pasturage for the 'rother beastes and horsebeastes' of the inhabitants and allowing access to all kinds of persons 'to walke, bowle, shute and otherwyse to use their lawfull disporte'[115] showing that the townsfolk used the area for all kinds of recreational activities.

The northward extent of the coneygar is not known, but it did not stretch as far as the 'Narrows'. Another lease of 1619 referred to a plot 'lying without the Cuniger on the west side of the highway towards the Narrows' which was granted for the erection of a windmill. Its southern limit is more problematic. The 1563 lease seems to imply that the warren was on both sides of the town ditch, whereas that of 1579 states that it was on the north side only. It may be that the town ditch actually served a dual purpose, both as warren limit and town boundary. It can scarcely have been a defensive feature. By 1617 it appears to have become a lane called Cuniger Ditch

In the reign of Elizabeth I there were growing signs of development. Weinstock notes a 'steady expansion of Melcombe'[116] with a significant turnover of properties in the area between St. Alban Street and the town ditch. According to a survey of holdings in Melcombe and Weymouth, made in 1617, in Melcombe there were 217 properties belonging to 135 separate owners. As one would expect, they were arranged around the streets of the original grid and along New Street, but extensions of St. Thomas Street and St. Mary Street had also by this time pushed out beyond the town ditch with some 30 house properties in this area[117]. On the other side of the harbour, in Weymouth, there were 241 properties concentrated on both sides of the High Street and around the Hope.

Gerard believed that by this time most of the town's merchants had 'chosen [Melcombe] for their habitation which of late years is fairly newly built'. Presumably they favoured Melcombe because its more extensive site was more convenient for warehousing etc., although it appears that by this time the most important merchants using the ports were Dorchester and other 'inland' men.

By the middle of the sixteenth century it was becoming clear, to some at least, that for the port to work efficiently there had to be unified control. This issue appeared more urgent because it seems that during the reign of Elizabeth I the old disputes over the harbour had accelerated and issues of governance were coming to a head. Some basics of agreement were sketched out and incorporated into an Exchequer Decree of 1564 towards this end. There was to be joint use of the harbour; the freemen of Melcombe were to have half of the petty customs collected in Weymouth; in return, the freemen of Weymouth were to have half of the cartage and of the rents of the 'watter mill' and the cuniger of Melcombe and the same trading privileges in Melcombe as Melcombe burgesses. Weymouth bailiffs, however, were to keep all the returns from 'bushellage' (duty on goods sold by the bushel) and the 'fee fish' (royal fish, due to the Queen as lord of the manor and part of the fee farm). Little of this was carried into effect, however, and the subsequent once and for all attempt to reform town government, the so-called 'Charter of Union' of 1571 was similarly ineffective. This united the two boroughs into a single corporation which was to have a mayor as its chief officer and justice of the peace, presiding over the borough court, and there were also to be two bailiffs[118]. This latter measure was to create new problems.

The existence of the two bailiffs was a clear concession to the Weymouth side and the Weymouth bailiffs clung on to their old liberties and privileges as officers of a royal manor to subvert the intentions of the new charter. They had already, in

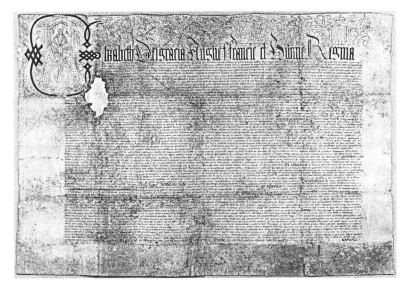

Weymouth 'Charter of Union', 1571
(DHC DWM CH1)
This 'charter' or order describes sixteenth century disputes between
the two boroughs and orders their union by implementing the Act
of Parliament to that effect.

1569, invoked the Royal Steward, the Earl of Pembroke, in an attempt to intimidate the Melcombe mayor. Now they persisted in holding a court leet and three-weekly 'law days' again under the Queen's Steward's authority. They claimed that Weymouth revenues properly belonged to the Queen and the crown added to these problems in 1575 by confirming to the royal manors of Wyke, Portland *and Weymouth* freedom from outside jurisdiction, including Admiralty. Repeated interventions by the Privy Council and the Court of Exchequer to attempt to sort things out proved either ineffective or actually unhelpful. On the one hand, the Court pronounced responses from the Weymouth bailiffs to be 'frivolous and dilatory' while, on the other authorising them to continue collecting 'for the Queen' the fee farm from Weymouth of about £10 and her entitlement of 40 shillings from the petty customs and also to carry on holding 'law days' because they were acting for her as lord of the manor[119].

It was for reasons like this that it took many years before the governance of the town could free itself from the relics of medieval practice. It was not until 1616 that these matters were finally cleared up by letters patent of James I. These tellingly declared that J. Roy is to become and be 'the first and modern mayor of the borough' (fore et esse primu et modernu maiorem burgis), Richard Pitt and ten others to be the 'first and modern Aldermen' and Peter Nettle and twenty three others to be the 'first and modern Principal or Capital Burgesses'[120].

This finally settled the issue of the government of the town by a single corporation. But something perhaps equally important had happened some years earlier. This was the building of a bridge which linked the two old towns and established a physical as well as

Letters Patent of James I, 1616
This document is the effective constitutional foundation of the
united boroughs. At its head a drawing of James I can be seen
inside the initial J of his name.

a constitutional union. This had been mooted as early as 1580 when at an Exchequer Court meeting representatives from the Weymouth side proposed that a bridge would be 'very beneficial... [to the]... burgesses, tenants and inhabitants of Weymouth and a great quiet unto both the said towns and inhabitants thereof, in respect of unity and quietness to be had and continued between them'[121]. From the Melcombe side the mayor, Thomas Howard, speaking for the new corporation, agreed and offered to pay 'two pence for every penny on the part of them of Weymouth' towards it if the assembly of the corporation agreed. In 1584 an attempt was made to raise a levy to build the bridge but without much success and in 1592 it fell to the Privy Council to urge the Dorset justices to try to secure contributions to the cost from wider afield in the county as a whole, on the grounds that it would be of general benefit. It seems that Londoners ultimately bore the largest proportion of the costs which amounted in total to 'neere upon 1000l'. The construction was under way in 1593 and by 1597 a wooden bridge with seventeen arches and a central drawbridge had been completed[122].

By the late sixteenth century, then, it can be seen that Weymouth was beginning to emerge from its medieval past. The governance of the two small towns was now unified under a single corporation. They were also, at last, physically joined together by a bridge. Hesitantly and uncertainly, the old ways were being left behind. But the medieval legacy was great and remains to this day. The modern street system clearly follows the pattern of the two old boroughs and ancient property boundaries – the burgage plots – continue to affect the fabric of the town. Weymouth is often described as being 'Georgian' in character. But obviously that is only half the story. Perhaps the town should have statues of Edward I and Eleanor of Castile, to mark their influence, as well as those of George III and Queen Victoria.

Seal of the combined boroughs, 1592
*This is an early seal of the combined boroughs. The impress is of
the 1592 coat of arms showing on the ship's foremast the arms
of England and on the mizzen the arms of Castile, references
to Edward I and Eleanor of Castile, the 'founders' of Melcombe.
On the hull are the arms of the Clare family, indicating their
association with Weymouth.*

Endnotes

1   Swanson, H., 1999, Medieval British Towns, Basingstoke

2   Sawyer, P.H., 1968, Anglo-Saxon Charters, London, no. 391

3   Mills, A.D., 1977, Place Names of Dorset, part 1, Cambridge, p. 250

4   Sawyer, op. cit., no. 938; Keynes, S., 1980, The Diplomas of King Aethelred the Unready, 978-1016, A Study in their Use as Historical Evidence, London, pp. 84, 268

5   Grundy, G.B., 1939, 'Saxon Charters of Dorset', Somerset and Dorset Notes and Queries, 61, pp.66-7, Henceforth SDNQ.

6   Hutchins, J., 1861-70, (eds.) Skipp,W. and Hodson, J.W., The History and Antiquities of the County of Dorset, 3rd edition, 4 vols., Westminster. Vol. II deals with Weymouth and Melcombe

7   Sawyer, loc. cit.

8   Ellis, G.A., 1829, The History and Antiquities of the Borough and Town of Weymouth and Melcombe Regis, Weymouth. Ellis recounts the details of all his with evident relish.

9   Hutchins, op. cit., p.428

10   See Swanson, op. cit., pp.2, 67-8

11   Beresford, M.W., 1967, New Towns of the Middle Ages: Town Plantation in England, Wales and Gascony, London, p.430

12   Beresford, op. cit.,p.430

13   Ellis, op. cit., pp.24-5

14   Moule, H.J., 1883, Descriptive Catalogue of the Charters, Minute Books and Other Documents of the Borough of Weymouth and Melcombe Regis, AD 1252-1800, Weymouth, pp.15-19

15 I am indebted to Mr. R. Samways for a copy of the latin text of this charter and a translation; also to Weymouth Museum

16 Weinbaum,M., 1943/2010, British Borough Charters, 1307-1660, Cambridge, pp. xliv,liv,xxiv, 31, 33

17 Hutchins, op. cit., pp. 472-8

18 Hutchins, op.cit., pp. 418,446

19 Coker, J., 1980, A Survey of Dorsetshire etc., 2nd. ed., Sherborne, p. 33

20 Leland, J, Itinerary, cited in Ellis, op. cit., pp. 10-11, 114

21 Ellis, op. cit., p. 10. See also the map in Royal Commission on Historical Monuments. An Inventory of the Historical Monuments of the County of Dorset, vol. II, South East, part 2, RCHM, HMSO, London

22 Moule, op. cit.,p. 16

23 Penn, K.J., 1980, Historic Towns in Dorset, (Dorset Archaeological Committee, DNHAS, Monograph Series no. 1), p. 119 and map

24 Beaton, D., 2001, Dorset Maps, Wimborne, p. 9

25 Beresford, op. cit., p. 426

26 Boyce, C., 1927-9, 'Ower. Vestiges of its History', SDNQ, vol. xix, pp. 207-8

27 Hutchins, op. cit., p. 448

28 Weinstock, M (n.d.), More Dorset Studies, map facing p.42

29 Pinches, S., 2010, Ledbury, People and Parish before the Reformation, Chichester

30 Mills, 1977, op.cit., p. 253

31 Weinstock, M., (n.d.), More Dorset Studies, Dorchester, map facing p. 22

32 Oliver,V.L.,1933, 'King Edward I and Melcombe Regis', PDNHAS, vol.55, pp. 32-3

33 Some details of this transfer are given in an Exemplification made for the burgesses of Weymouth in 1367. Fifth Report of the Royal Commission on Historical Manuscripts, Part 1, Report and Appendix, 1876, London, Cmd., p.575. Henceforth RCHMa

34 Altschul, M., 1965, A Baronial Family in Medieval England:the Clares 217-1314, Baltimore, p.258

35 Palliser, D.M., Slater, T.R.and Dennison, E.P., 2000, 'The Topography of English Towns' in Palliser, D., ed., Cambridge Urban History of Britain, 600-1540, vol.1, Cambridge, p.168

36 Ellis, op. cit., p.87

37 Hutchins, op. cit., p.449

38 Mills, A.D., ed., 1971, 'The Dorset Lay Subsidy, 1332', Dorset Record Society, 4, Dorchester

39 Beresford,1967, op.cit., p.67

40 According to Campbell, B.M.S.,2008, 'Benchmarking medieval economic development:England, Wales, Scotland and Ireland c.1290', Economic History Review, vol.61,no. 4, 'probably the most straightforward basis for comparing the relative trades of individual ports c. 1290 is in terms of the respective customs revenues that were generated, reckoning these revenues at £0.33 sterling per sack of wool, per 300 woolfells and per half last of hides'. Using figures based on Jenks, S., ed., 2004, The Enrolled Customs accounts, List and Index Society, Kew, he shows that in 1289-90, in a list of 14 head ports, the 7 southern and western ports of Chichester, Weymouth/Poole, Seaford, Yarmouth, Exeter and Bristol contributed together merely £193 or 1.9% of English customs revenue. By comparison Boston contributed £3,361 (32.7%), London £3,241 (31.5%), Hull £1,289 (12.5%), Southampton £871 (8.5%) and Lynn £522 (5.1%).

41   McKisack, M., 1959, The Fourteenth Century, 1307-1399, Oxford, p.354

42   Penn, op.cit., p.115

43   Page, W., ed., 1908,The Victoria County History of Dorset. vol. II, London, p. 187. Henceforth VCH

44   Beresford, 1967, op. cit., p.254

45   Beresford, 1967, op. cit., pp.182,191

46   VCH, p.186. See also Kowaleski, M., ed., 1993, The Local Customs Accounts of the Port of Exeter, 1266-1321, Devon and Cornwall Record Society, new ser., 36, Exeter, who notes that coastal trade accounted for 70% of all Exeter's shipping traffic in the late thirteenth and early fourteenth centuries. See also Platt, C., 1973, Medieval Southampton, London, pp.157-163 on the nature and problems of coastal shipping in the fifteenth century.

47   Calendar of Inquisitions Miscellaneous, vol. VII (1399-1422), HMSO, 1968, London. Henceforth CIM

48   Based on Mills, A.D., 1971, op. cit., pp.xii, 103-4

49   Platt, 1973, op.cit., p.264

50   Ellis, op. cit., p.148; Hutchins, op. cit., p.450

51   Flatman, J.,2009,Ships and Shipping in Medieval Manuscripts, London, makes the point,however, that there is no archaeological evidence for them, only documentary and iconographic (including other town seals at the time). The ship on the Melcombe seal could be a stylised representation.

52   Rodger, N.A.M.,2004, The Safeguard of the Sea, A Naval History of Britain, 660-1649, London, pp.61-72. See also Sherborne, J.W., 1977, 'English Barges and Balyngers of the late 14th. century', Mariners Mirror, lxiii, pp.109-14

53   VCH, p. 184

54   VCH, p.186

55   Ellis, op.cit., p.114

56 Horrox, R., ed., 1994, The Black Death, Manchester'
    contains references to the following chronicles: Gransden,
    A., ed., 1957, 'A Fourteenth Century Chronicle from
    the Greyfriars at Lyn', English Historical Review, LXII,
    p.274; Haydon, F.S., ed., 1863, Eulogium Historiarum sive
    Temporis, vol. III, Rolls Series (henceforth RS), London,
    pp. 213-14; Thomson, E.M., ed., 1889, Robertus de
    Avesbury de Gestis Mirabilitibus Regis Edwardi Tertii,
    RS

57 Lumby, J.R., ed., 1895, Chronicon Henrici Knighton vel
    Cnitthon monachi Leycestrensis, vol.II, RS., pp. 58-65.

58 Register of Bishop Ralph of Shrewsbury, Somerset Record
    Society, X, 1896, pp. 555-6

59 Thomson, E.M., ed., 1889, Chronicon Galfridi le Baker
    de Swynebroke, Oxford, pp. 92,98-100

60 Fletcher, J.M., 1923, 'The Black Death in Dorset', PDNHAS,
    XLIII

61 Rodger, op. cit., p. 91

62 Sumption, J., The Hundred Years War, vol.1, Trial by Battle,
    London, pp. 346-7

63 VCH, pp.185-6

64 VCH, p.187

65 VCH, pp.188-90

66 Johnes,T.,1803, Sir John Froissart's Chronicles of England,
    France and the Adjoining Countries from the latter part
    of the reign of Edward II to the Coronation of Henry IV,
    newly translated by Thomas Johnes, vol.II, p. 181. I have
    slightly edited this passage. Johnes translates French and
    Spanish titles into English

67 VCH, p. 187

68 Hutchins, op.cit., p.449

69 Ellis, op.cit., pp. 146-7

70 This text is taken from the original (Pynson edition) of 1523 of The first volum of Sir Johan Froyssart; of the cronycles of Englande, Fraunce, Spayne, Portyngale, Scotlande, Bretayne, Flauders and other places adjoynynge. Traslated out of frenche into our maternall englysshe tonge by J. Bourchier, etc., cap. xxxvii

71 CIM, 1968, vol.VII, (1399-1422), pp. 196-7

72 Moule, op. cit., VI

73 Hutchins, op. cit., vol.I, p.1

74 VCH, p. 192

75 Hutchins, op. cit., vol.II, p. 419

76 Forrest, M., 2013, 'Economic Changes in Late Medieval Dorset; an analysis of evidence from the lay subsidies', PDNHAS, vol. 134, pp. 68-82

77 Moule, op. cit., p. 4

78 Astle, T. et al., op. cit

79 Hutchins, op. cit., p.456; Ellis, op. cit., pp. 173-4

80 VCH, p. 19

81 VCH, p. 19

82 Penn, op. cit., p. 115

83 Ellis, op. cit., p. 98

84 RCHMa, p. 577

85 VCH, p. 92

86 VCH, pp. 19-20

87 VCH, p. 92; Ellis, op. cit., pp. 164-5; Hutchins, op. cit., p. 454

88 VCH, p. 93

89 Payne, D., 1953, Dorset Harbours, London, p. 70.

90 Beaton, op. cit., pp. 9,10, 14. The originals are in the British Library

91 Ellis, op. cit., p. 98

92 Ellis, op. cit., p. 98

93 Ellis, op. cit., p. 99

94   Fry, E.A., 1908, 'Dorset Chantries', PDNHAS, vol. 29, pp. 42-3

95   Fry, op. cit., p. 43

96   RCHMa., pp. 575, 578

97   Ellis, op. cit., p. 221

98   Details of the granting of markets and fairs to Weymouth and Melcombe can be found in CCR, 1226-57 p.351 and CCR 1300-26 pp.274, 375

99   Ellis, op. cit., p. 25

100   Dyer, C., 2009, Making a Living in the Middle Ages. The People of Britain, 850-1520, London, pp. 298-9

101   Hutchins, op. cit., pp. 450-1

102   Hunt, J.J. and Dawe, P.N., eds., 1955, 'A Dorset Lay Subsidy Roll, 1525', SDNQ,vol.xxvi, pp. 204-8 and vol. xxvii , 1961, p. 28

103   Stoate, T. L., ed.,1978, Dorset Tudor Muster Rolls, 1539, 1542,1569, Bristol

104   Hunt and Dawe, op. cit., p.28

105   Weinstock, M., 1953, Studies in Dorset History, Dorchester, pp. 30-2.

106   Coker, op. cit., p. 35.

107   Weinstock, 1953, op. cit., p. 28

108   Weinstock, 1953, op. cit., p. 48

109   Stephens, W.B., 1974, 'The Trade Fortunes of Poole, Weymouth and Lyme Regis, 1600-1640', PDNHAS, vol. 95, pp. 71-3

110   Weinstock, 1953, op. cit., p. 43

111   Carter, H., 1976, 'The Town in its Setting. The Geographical Approach' in Barley, M.W., ed., The Plans and Topography of Medieval Towns in England and Wales, Council for British Archaeology, Research Report no. 14, London

112   Weinstock, n.d., op. cit., p21

113   Mills, 1977, op. cit., p. 251

114   British Library, Cott. Mss. Augustus,I,32

115   Moule, op. cit., p.93

116   Weinstock, n.d., op. cit., p. 21

117   Moule, op. cit., p.p. 105-6

118   Hutchins, op. cit., p. 429

119   All of this is gone into in some detail in Hutchins, Appendix H, pp.472-8

120   Moule, op. cit., p.9.

121   Hutchins, op. cit., p. 476

122   Weinstock, n.d., p.37

Abbreviations

CCR	Calendar of Charter Rolls
CIM	Calendar of Inquisitions Miscellaneous
CPR	Calendar of Patent Rolls
DHC	Dorset History Centre
EHR	English Historical Review
Ec.HR	Economic History Review
EPNS	English Place Name Society
PDNHA	Proceedings of the Dorset Natural History and Archaeological Society
RS	Rolls Series
SDNQ	Somerset and Dorset Notes and queies
VCH	Victoria County History

Bibliography

Allmand, C.T., *The Hundred Years War:England and France at War c.1300-c.1450* (Cambridge, 1988)

Altschul, M., *A Baronial Family in Medieval England:The Clares, 1217-1314* (Baltimore, 1965)

Arkell, T.,'Multiplying Factors for Estimating Population Totals from the Hearth Tax' *Local Population Studies*, 28,1982

Astle, T., Ayscough, S. and Caley, J. (eds), *Taxatio Ecclesiastica Angliae et Walliae Auctoritate Papae Nicholai IV* 1291-2, Record Commission (London 1802)

Attwooll,M. and West, J., *Weymouth. An Illustrated History* (Wimborne 1995)

Barley, M.W., (ed.), The Plans and Topography of Medieval Towns in England and Wales, *Council for British Archaeology Research Report No. 14* (London 1976)

Beaton, D., *Dorset Maps* (Wimborne 2001)

Beresford, M.W., *New Towns of the Middle Ages:Town Plantation in England, Wales and Gascony* (London 1967)

Beresford, M.W., History on the Ground (London 1971)

Blair, J., 'Small Towns:600-1270', in Palliser,D.,(ed.) *Cambridge Urban History of Britain:600-1540*,vol.1 (Cambridge 2000)

Boyce, C., 'Ower. Vestiges of its History', *SDNQ* XIX (1927-9)

Bourchier, Sir J., Lord Berners, *The Chronicles of Froissart* (Pynson edition) (London 1523-5)

Bridbury, A.R., *Economic Growth. England in the Later Middle Ages* (London 1962)

Butler, L., 'The Evolution of Towns after 1066' in Barley, M.W. (ed.) (1976)

Calendar of Inquisitions Miscellaneous vol.VII 1399-1422 (London 1968)

Campbell, B.M.S., 'Benchmarking medieval economic development. England, Wales, Scotland and Ireland c. 1290', *Ec.H.R.* vol.61, no.4, 2008

Carter, H., 'The Town in its setting. The Geographical Approach' in Barley, M.W. (ed.) 1976

Coker, J., *A Survey of Dorsetshire* etc ,2nd. ed.,(Sherborne 1980)

Conzen, M.R.G., 'The Use of Town Plans in the Study of Urban History' in Dyos, H.J., 1968

Curry, A., *The Hundred Years War 1337-1453* (Oxford 2002)

Dyer, A., *Decline and Growth in English Towns 1400-1640* (Cambridge 1995)

Dyer, C., *Making a Living in the Middle Ages. The People of Britain, 850-1520* (London 2009)

Dyos, H.J., *The Study of Urban History* (London 1968)

Ellis, G.A., *The History and Antiquities of the Borough and Town of Weymouth and Melcombe Regis* (Weymouth 1829)

Fifth Report of the Royal Commission on Historical Manuscripts. Pt.1. *Report and Appendix* (London 1876)

Flatman, J., *Ships and Shipping in Medieval Manuscripts* (London 2009)

Fletcher, J.M., 'The Black Death in Dorset', *PDNHAS* XLIII (1923)

Forrest,M., 'Economic Change in Late Medieval Dorset:An Analysis of Evidence from the Lay Subsidies', *PDNHAS* vol. 134 (2013)

Friel,I., *The Good Ship:Ships, Shipbuilding and Technology in England 1200-1520* (London 1995)

Fry, E.A., 'Dorset Chantries', *PDNHAS*,vol.29 (1908)

Good,R., Weyland. *The Story of Weymouth and its Countryside* (Dorchester 1946)

Grundy, G.B., 'Saxon Charters of Dorset', *SDNQ*, 61 (1939)

Horrox,R., *The Black Death. Manchester Medieval Sources Series.* (Manchester 1955)

Hunt,J.J. and Dawe,P.N., (eds.) 'A Dorset Lay Subsidy Roll', *SDNQ*, XXVI and XXVII (1955/1961)

Hutchins, J., (eds. W. Skipp and J.W. Hodson) *The History and Antiquities of the County of Dorset*, 3rd.ed.,4 vols. (Westminster 1861-70)

Jenks,S., (ed.) *The Enrolled Customs Accounts*. List and Index Society (Kew 2004)

Johnes,T., (ed.) *Sir John Froissart's Chronicles of England, France and the adjoining Countries from the latter part of the reign of Edward II to the Coronation of Henry V*.(London 1803-1810)

Ker,W.P., (ed.) *The Chronicles of Froissart* (This is an edition of Berners' translation.) (London 1901-3)

Keynes,S., as *The Diplomas of King Aethelred the Unready. A Study in their Use Historical Evidence.*(London 1980)

Koweleski,M., (ed.) *The Local Customs Accounts of the Port of Exeter 1266-1321*, Devon and Cornwall Record Society, New ser. 36 (Exeter 1993)

Long, E.T., 'The Religious Houses of Dorset', *PDNHAS* vol.53 (1931)

McKisack,M., *The Fourteenth Century* (Oxford 1959)

Mills,A.D., *The Dorset Lay Subsidy 1332*, Dorset Record Society 4 (1971)

Mills,A.D., *Place Names of Dorset*,pt.1, EPNS (Cambridge 1977)

Moule, H.J. (ed.) *Descriptive Catalogue of the Charters, Minute Books and other Documents of the Borough of Weymouth and Melcombe Regis, 1251-1800* (Weymouth 1883)

Oliver, V.L., 'King Edward I and Melcombe Regis', *PDNHAS*. vol.55 (1933)

Ottaway,P., *Archaeology in British Towns. From the Emperor Claudius to the Black Death* (London 1992)

Page, W., (ed.) *The Victoria County History of Dorset* vol.II (London 1908)

Palliser,D.M., Slater, T.R. and Dennison, E.P. 'The Topography of English Towns in Palliser, D. (ed.) *Cambridge Urban History of Britain:600-1540*, vol 1 (Cambridge 200)

Payne, D., *Dorset Harbours* (London 1953)

Penn, K.J., *Historic Towns in Dorset*, Dorset Archaeological Committee, DNHAS Monograph Series no.1 (1980)

Pinches, S., Ledbury. *People and Parish before the Reformation* (Chichester 2010)

Platt, C.P.S., *Medieval Southampton:the Port and Trading Community* (London 1973)

Platt, C., *The English Medieval Town* (London 1976)

Platt, C., *King Death. The Black Death and its aftermath in late-medieval England* (Toronto 1997)

Rigby, S.H., 'Late Medieval Urban Prosperity:The Evidence of the Lay Subsidies' *Ec.H.R.* 2nd ser. XXXIX, 3 (1986)

Rodger, N.A.M., *The Safeguard of the Sea. A Naval History of Britain, 660-1649* (London 1987)

Royal Commission on Historical Manuscripts. *Fifth Report*, Part 1 Report and Appendix (London 1876)

Royal Commission on Historical Monuments. *An Inventory of the Historical Monuments of the County of Dorset* vol. II, South-East Part 2 (London 1970)

Sawyer, P.H., *Anglo-Saxon Charters* (London 1968)

Schurer, K. and Arkell, T., (eds.), Surveying the People (Oxford 1992)

Sherborne, J.W., 'English Barges and Balyngers of the late 14th. century', *Mariners Mirror*,lxiii (1977)

Slater, T.R., 'The South West of England', Palliser, D.,(ed.) *Cambridge Urban History of Britain 600-1540*, vol.1 (Cambridge 2000)

Stoate, T.L., (ed.) *Dorset Tudor Muster Rolls, 1539, 1542, 1569* (Bristol 1978)

Stephens, W.B., 'The Trade Fortunes of Poole, Weymouth and Lyme Regis, 1600-1640', *PDNHAS,* vol.95 (1974)

Sumption, J., *Trial by Fire. The Hundred Years War II* (London 2001)

Swanson, H., *Medieval British Towns* (Basingstoke 1999)

Tait, J., *The Medieval English Borough. Studies on its Origins and Constitutional History* (Manchester 1968)

Tinniswood, J.T., 'English Galleys, 1272-1377' *Mariners Mirror*, XXXV (1949)

Weinbaum, M., *British Borough Charters 1307 - 1660* (Cambridge 2010)

Weinstock, M., *Studies in Dorset History* (Dorchester 1953)

Weinstock, M., *More Dorset Studies* (Dorchester n.d.)

Williamson, T., *The Archaeology of Rabbit Warrens* (Princes Risborough, 2006)

Wrigley, E.A. and Schofield, R.S., *The Population History of England 1541-1871.*

A Reconstruction 2nd. ed. (Cambridge 1989)

Index

A

Abbot, John 65
Abbot, William 72
Act of Resumption 59
Aethelred II 5
Ale 12, 15, 63, 66-67, 69
Alwyn, bishop of Winchester 6
Anglo-Saxon Charters 4
Assize of ale 12, 66, 69
Athelstan 4

B

Backwater 4, 59, 77
Bailiffs 12, 15, 18, 28, 44, 63-69, 72, 80-81
Bakerestrete 17, 24, 26
Balyngers 35-37
Barges 35-37, 44-45, 50
Bayonne 8
Bincombe 41
Black Death 1, 38-40, 42
Black Friars 56
Bond Street 27
Books of Institutions 40
Bordeaux 8, 39
Boroughs 3, 9-10, 18, 73, 80-84
Bourchier, Sir John, 48, 90, 93
Bourneuf Bay 45
Bridge 3, 82-83
Bristol 37-39

Brittany 43, 45
Burgage plots 11, 25, 29, 31, 83
Burgage tenure 11
Burgesses 10-12, 14, 17, 20, 25, 28, 31, 48-50, 53, 60-61, 63, 71-73, 80, 82-83, 87

C

Calais 32, 37, 45
Calche, Robert 65
Cerne Abbey 7
Chandler, John, bishop of Salisbury 57
Chantry 61
Chapel 54-58, 60-62, 68
Chapelhay Steps 55
Chapell of St George 62
Charles V, King of France 46
Charles VI, King of France 47
Charter of Union 80-81
Charters v, vii, 1, 4, 9-10, 15, 18, 28, 31
Chickerell 29, 41
Churchyards 41
Cinque Ports 43-44
Clare family, Earls of Gloucester 4, 28, 31, 33, 84
Clergy 39-41, 58
Clopton, Walter 65
Clos de Gallees, Rouen 46
Cloth 8, 32-33, 65, 77

Cogs 36
Coker, John 22, 86, 91, 94
Cole, Thomas 72
Compostela 35, 52
Coneybery Hills 78
Coneys 78-79
Corpus Christi Day, festival of 60-61
Court 10, 12, 14, 28, 50, 56-57, 63-72, 80-81, 83
Court of Exchequer 81
Courts of Assize - 9
Cuniger 79-80
Cuniger Ditch 79
Customs 6, 11-12, 15, 18, 20, 32-34, 49-51, 58-59, 64, 77, 80-81, 87-88, 95

D

Dartmouth 46
Deer, Hugh 64, 65
Depe (Dieppe) 47-48
Deverell, Hugh 56-57, 60
Domesday Book 5, 6-7
Dominicans 56-57, 60
Dorchester 4, 41, 63, 65, 77, 80
Durnovaria 4

E

Edward I 4, 5-6, 12-13, 18, 19, 23-24, 31 33, 35, 43-6, 54, 83-84
Edward II 5, 12-13, 16, 31, 44, 46

Edward III 18-19, 32-33, 43, 45-46, 49, 83
Edward the Confessor 5
Elizabeth I 79-80
Exchequer Court 14, 81, 83
Exchequer Decree 80

F

Fairs 9, 70, 91
Fee farm 17, 19-20, 31, 48-49, 52, 71-74, 80-81
Ferry 3, 23
Forde, Henry 64
Fox, Roger 64, 69
France 1, 8, 32, 37, 39, 42-43, 46-47, 53, 71, 76, 89, 93, 95
Franchise Street 30
Fraternity of St. George 60, 62
Friars 38, 56-60
Friary 4, 10, 11, 12, 24, 57-59
Friary Lane 58
Froissart, Jean 46, 48, 89, 93, 95

G

Galleys 43-44
Gascony 8, 24, 39, 43, 52
Gerard, Thomas 22, 25, 76, 80
Gloucester 64
Guild of St. George of Weymouth, see Fraternity of St. George

H

Hellier, William 64, 65, 67
Henry I 6, 8, 35, 60
Henry II 7-8
Henry III 24
Henry IV 35, 48-49, 64, 71, 89
Henry V 45, 95
Henry VI 53, 59-60, 73
Henry VII 53, 74
Henry VIII 53, 59, 74
High Street 29-30, 55, 79
Hope Square 11
Hopehus 11, 23
Howard, Thomas 83
Hundred Years War 1, 43, 89,
    93-94, 96
Hutchins, John 85-86, 88, 91, 95

I

Impressment 45, 52
Incorporation 18
Inquisitions 18, 20, 34, 49, 64, 70

J

James I 82
Jetty 59-60
Jews 15

K

Kemer, Eustace 64-65
King John 43
Knighton, Henry 39, 41-42,
    61, 89

L

Langynow, Richard 35
Lay Subsidies 53, 74, 90, 94, 96
Leland, John 22-23, 38, 53, 58,
    75, 86
Letters Patent of James I 82
Lodmoor 5
Lok, John 57
Love Lane 30
Lowen, John 57
Lower St. Alban Street 27
Lower St. Edmund Street 23,
    25
Lyme Regis 5, 91, 96

M

Maiden Street 26-27, 58, 68
Maior, Barnarde 79
Manors 6-7, 81
Market Place 22, 24-26, 29-30
Markets 9, 33, 63, 70, 72, 91
Melcombe Charter 9, 12-14,
    16, 18-19, 21, 24, 85
Milton Abbey 4
Morton, John 57
Muster roll 74

N

Narrows 27, 60, 79
Netley Abbey 33, 71
New Street 79
Newfoundland 76-77
Newton 23

Normandy 8, 43, 48, 52-53

Normans 76

O

Owermoigne 41

P

Parliament 3, 32, 36, 48, 50, 59, 64-65, 72-73, 81

Peacekeeping 69

Petticoat Lane 27

Piepowder court 69

Pitt, Richard 82

Plantagenets 19

Plymouth 34, 37, 44, 46

Pog 46

Poldyng, Edward 57

Poole 34, 37, 44-46, 50-52, 56, 59, 72, 76-77

Pope Martin V 57

Pope Nicholas IV 54

Portesham 31-32, 41

Portland 5-6, 28, 31, 59-61, 78, 81

Portsmouth 11-12, 43-44, 46

Privy Council 81, 83

Processions 39, 60-61

Q

Quay 24, 27, 29, 68

Queen Eleanor 4, 19, 28, 84

Queen Emma 5-6

R

Radipole 4, 7, 24, 29, 41, 54-55, 57-59

Radipole Lake 4

Raids 43-44, 46, 67

Raynolde, Owen 76

Register of Bishop Ralph of Shrewsbury 89

Richard II 11, 23, 46, 48-49, 71

Ridgeway 11, 70

River Wey 5, 29, 70

Rogers, John 56-57, 60, 72

Roy, John 82

Russell, Henry 46, 61-62, 68

Rye 46

S

Samwise, Robert 76

Seals v, 16, 19, 36, 62, 67, 84, 88

Ships 15, 18, 35-37, 39, 43-46, 50, 52, 66, 76, 88, 94

Shoydon, Henry 35, 76

Shudde, John 56, 66-68

Sluys, battle of iv, 44, 47

Southampton 11-12, 32, 37-39, 43-44, 46, 48, 51

Spain 35, 76

St. Alban Street 17, 26-27, 58, 77, 79

St. Botolph's fair 17, 71

St. Edmund Street 17, 23-26

St. Mary Street 17, 24, 26-27, 79

St. Nicholas Street   23, 26-27, 55-56, 60

St. Thomas Street   17, 24, 26-27, 79

Staple   32-33, 51

Stapleware   51

Studland   23

T

Taunton, William of   9, 10, 28

Taxatio Ecclesiastica   54, 93

Town ditch   17, 24, 27-28, 77-79

Town hall   29-30

Trajectus   23

U

Upwey   55

V

Vico Sancti Nicolai   27

W

Wales   24, 54

Walkelyn, William   67

Walter de Marisco   24

War   vii, 1, 36-38, 43-44, 56, 89, 93-94, 96

Wareham   33, 37, 45

Warmwell   41

Warren   78-79

Welyfed, Cristina   76

West Chaldon   41

West Chickerell   29, 41

West Knighton   41

West Stafford   41

Westminster   64-65

Wey   4-5, 29, 51, 70

Weybause   55

Weymouth Charter   v, 5, 9-10, 14, 20-21, 23, 80-81, 85

Winchester Cathedral   4, 6

Winchester Old Minster   5-6

Wine trade   8, 33, 52

Winterborne Came   41

Winterborne Monkton   41

Wool   1, 8, 31-33, 41, 44, 87

Wool trade   32-33

Wooton   61

Wyke   5, 6, 8-9, 29, 35, 54-55, 60-62, 81